Speaker of the House

Speaker of the House
*The Political Career and Times of
John L. O'Brien*

Daniel Jack Chasan

UNIVERSITY OF WASHINGTON PRESS
Seattle and London

Library of Congress Cataloging in Publication Data

Chasan, Daniel Jack.
    Speaker of the House: the political career and times of John L.
    O'Brien/Daniel Jack Chasan.
        p. cm.
    Bibliography: p.
    Includes index.
    ISBN 0-295-96848-6
    1. O'Brien, John L.   2. Legislators—Washington (State)—Biog-
raphy.   3. Washington (State). Legislature. House of Representatives—Biography.   4. Washington (State). Legislature. House of Representatives—Speaker—Biography.   5. Washington (State)—Politics
and government—1951–   I. Title. F895.22.027C47 1990
328.797′092—dc20
[B]   89-35317
                                                                  CIP

ISBN 0-295-96848-6

∞

Contents

Foreword

MANY PEOPLE DESERVE SPECIAL RECOGNITION AND thanks for their support and encouragement during my political career. First and foremost, I wish to honor the memory of my beloved parents, James Thomas and Mary Margaret O'Brien, and I thank my loving wife, Mary, and our children, Laurie, John L., Jr., Mary Ann, Karen, Jeannie, and Paul, who shared with me so many triumphs and trials. Because of their belief in me and the people of Washington State, I was able to dedicate much of my life to public service.

For her many years of assistance in my Olympia office, Mary Walker deserves recognition for her help as my Administrative Assistant.

I gratefully acknowledge the efforts of:

The Honorable Richard "Doc" Hastings who, with a keen interest in the history of the Washington State Legislature and Washington State, encouraged me to share and record my knowledge of state government and legislative experiences. This resolution, of which he was the prime sponsor, was adopted by the House of Representatives in 1982;

The Honorable Brian Ebersole, who demonstrated a warm interest in my legislative career and the recording of it;

Stanley O. McNaughton, who was most generous with his efforts and time in assistance;

R. Mort Frayn, who was most helpful in the references to the history of the Washington House of Representatives;

Wilbert F. Lewis, who, at the district level, rendered invaluable assistance in furthering my services as a legislator;

All the lawmakers, House of Representatives staff, and citizens with whom I've toiled and triumphed for nearly half of Washington's years of statehood;

Daniel Jack Chasan, author of this book, who turned my memories and words into a historic reflection of the Washington State Legislature.

To all, Slainta! An Irish toast to your good health.

JOHN L. O'BRIEN

Speaker of the House
The Political Career and Times of John L. O'Brien

I

Stately Hotels and Depression-Era Politics

THE LEGISLATORS, THEIR JACKETS AND TIES RUMPLED after a bitter debate that had already lasted into dinner-time, were on their feet, screaming. The Speaker, a tall, immaculately dressed man with dark-framed glasses and thinning hair, banged his gavel down so hard that pencils and papers flew into the air. Then he turned on his heel and walked out. On the floor of the Washington State House of Representatives, people were still shouting, waving, milling about. The opposition, knowing that the Speaker's side lacked a majority, wanted the debate to continue. But the Speaker did not return. The filibuster of 1961 was the emotional climax of a war that had raged in Washington State and in the legislature for thirty-five years, the turning point in a battle that, a quarter century later, some seasoned politicians would call the most dramatic event of their political lives. By cutting off debate on House Bill 197, Speaker John L. O'Brien had just saved the day for his side.

O'Brien could not know it at the time, but that victory marked the apex of his power in the House. His days as Speaker would soon be over. His days in the House would not. Twenty-four years later, in 1985, no longer Speaker

3

but often called on to preside as Speaker pro tempore, John O'Brien sat at his oak desk in the front row of the marble-walled House chamber and listened as his colleagues unanimously passed a resolution honoring him for having served more than forty years in the House, and for having occupied leadership positions in a house of state government longer than anyone else in the United States.

O'Brien had served as Speaker—a powerful and controversial Speaker—for a record four terms between 1955 and 1963. He was serving his sixth term as Speaker pro tem, which allowed him to preside whenever the Speaker was not on the rostrum. Many of the House rules were rules he had made. He had been tutoring freshmen legislators in parliamentary procedure for years. "When I went there in '71," said Albert Bauer, a leader in the House who by 1985 had switched over to the state senate, "he was the guy who advised the freshman. He was the Socrates of the institution."

Socrates or not, the legislator who introduced the resolution in O'Brien's honor, Brian Ebersole, had heard when he entered the House in 1983 that the former Speaker was too old to be effective. He figured it might be true. Then, at the end of the session, when the House was struggling to pass a budget, Ebersole saw O'Brien at his best. The legislature worked on the budget all night. O'Brien was on the rostrum the whole time. Ebersole saw him "up there presiding all night when people half his age were down in their chairs asleep." The freshman legislator was convinced: the man who once was Speaker could still run the House.

O'Brien always had been at his best on the rostrum. He felt more alive there. He was tuned in. "On the rostrum," unlike on the floor of the House, he once said, "you can kind of get a *feel* for what's going to happen." He also got a burst of competitive energy. "When you go out there," he said, "you want to do the best you can. It's like playing golf: you want to go for a hole in one."

He had been at it for a long time. Ebersole had been elected just three years before. Only eight of his colleagues had been sitting there as long ago as 1973. O'Brien, however, had been elected in 1940 and, with one two-year break, had served ever since. He had, in fact, served almost half the time Washington had been a state. Since early legislatures met briefly and infrequently—even when he was first elected, a sixty-day session every two years was the norm—and later ones met more often and stayed longer, he had served more than half the days the legislature had actually met.

O'Brien had focused on the Speakership from the start. Becoming Speaker, being Speaker, and then being Speaker pro tem had absorbed his energies. It was not the issues per se that attracted him. It was presiding. As he said, "I've always worked at it on the basis that this was going as far as I possibly could in the legislature."

Being close to the rostrum had nevertheless put him close to a lot of the issues. Not ideological himself, as Speaker he became an enemy of the far right and a champion of the populist public power movement. As Speaker pro tem he was there to take the reins when one Speaker was toppled by rebellion and another was toppled by scandal.

Some people who had taken part in the earlier events were still in politics, but they were no longer in the House. O'Brien's commitment to the House and the rostrum was unique. In a body with few members who had served more than six years, he provided an institutional memory.

O'Brien himself tended to say that not much had changed—that politics was people, and people stayed the same. But the style and context of politics *had* changed. Few of the people who voted for Ebersole's resolution honoring O'Brien could recall a time when committee meetings were closed to the public, bills were routinely passed without public hearings, and committee membership depended solely on the Speaker's whim. Fewer still could recall a time when providing an old-age pension of $40 a month seemed a radical idea. O'Brien had served for decades while meetings were closed and the Speaker's word was law. He had entered the House when a $40 old-age pension was a burning issue. The House that honored O'Brien in 1985 had a different frame of reference from the House to which he was elected in 1940. He was an ambassador from a different world.

When John L. O'Brien was elected on November 5, 1940, Europe was already at war. The Battle of Britain was at its height. The British, trying to forestall an invasion of their island, were bombing invasion-takeoff points in the Low Countries. America was not yet involved. Washington, like the rest of the United States, was still living through the last days of the New Deal and the Great Depression.

The main event in that year's election was Franklin D. Roosevelt's battle for an unprecedented third term. It was not much of a battle. Roosevelt buried his opponent, Wendell Willkie. In Washington State, two young Democratic politicians, Warren Magnuson and Henry M. Jackson, later to become the most powerful pair of senators in the country, were running for Congress, Magnuson for his third term, Jackson for his first. The "good-government" Republican mayor of Seattle, Arthur B. Langlie, who had won his last election by a landslide without campaigning, was running for governor against former United States Senator Clarence Dill. And Democrat Monrad C. (Mon) Wallgren, talking incessantly about the Federal Columbia River dams and the New Deal, was running for the United States Senate against isolationist Stephen F. Chadwick.

It was hard to escape the campaign. On the Friday night before the election, Langlie was speaking on Seattle radio stations KOL-KMO and KVI at 8:00 and 10:30, Jackson was speaking on KOL at 6:30, and another radio station was advertising: "Too much politics?—Get more music and news on KRSC."

In the 33rd Legislative District, a largely ethnic, blue-collar area in south Seattle, one of the three Democratic candidates was a young, bespectacled accountant named John L. O'Brien. The Democrats running with him included an up-and-coming young state senator named Albert Rosellini, later to win two terms as Washington's governor, and H. C. (Army) Armstrong—his name was almost always written that way—part of the radical group in the state House of Representatives. (Rating candidates for the 1940 primary, the Seattle Municipal League said, "his record in legislature uniformly left-wing.")

The year before, after a conservative Democratic 33rd District representative, Harry Austin, died in office, O'Brien won an election held by the district's Democratic precinct committeemen to choose Austin's successor. The King County commissioners appointed him to the seat, but since the 1939 session of the legislature had already ended, he had not served a single day at the state capitol in Olympia.

Now, in November 1940, the election was almost anticlimactic. The 33rd District, like many other working-class Irish and Italian neighborhoods, was solidly Democratic. The only real question was who would get the Democratic nominations. O'Brien had won his by going around the district and talking to people one at a time. It was all a matter of personal contacts and commitments. The district "consisted of many Irish and Italian families and other ethnic groups at that time," he said later, "and we had a lot of friends and precinct committeemen who would take me around the neighborhood and introduce me to people."

They knew his mother, who was active in the church. They remembered his father, who had been a policeman. Younger people might remember O'Brien himself. He had been the one who sold hot dogs for school lunches and worked in a neighborhood grocery. He had been the one who gave out free passes for the neighborhood theater to kids who delivered theatrical news. Later, he had acted in amateur productions and served as business manager of the parish theatrical group.

He was already a successful young man: he had an accounting business; he had just started the American Oil Company, a home-heating business ("It looked to me like people were changing from coal to oil," he said later, "so I started it."); he was chairman of the Rainier District Pow Wow, a community summer festival replete with music, athletics, and pie-eating and beauty contests.

O'Brien had lived in the district all his life. He still lived with his mother in the frame house at 4209 Findlay Street that his father, an Irish immigrant police detective, had built twenty years before. James O'Brien had come to the United States from Ireland in 1905, six years before his first child, John, was born. He joined the police force four years later and became a detective in 1915. He built the house on Findlay Street in the summer of 1920. The following January, trying to arrest a cop killer in downtown Seattle, he was shot through the heart. John was not yet ten years old.

The trouble started on Friday night, January 21, near the corner of Broadway and Republican Street on Seattle's Capitol Hill, when a solitary young man named John Schmitt, referred to in some accounts as "the man in the mackinaw," opened fire on two patrolmen, wounding both of them fatally. Other cops started looking all over the city for the gunman. O'Brien and his long-time partner, T. G. Montgomery, were looking along Second Avenue. Near the Hoge Building at Second and Cherry they found their man. "Stop!" Montgomery shouted. "We are police officers. We want to look you over." Schmitt pulled a pistol from his pocket and fired at them. The first bullet passed through James O'Brien's heart. Montgomery emptied his gun at Schmitt, then ran at him and knocked him down.

When other policemen went to the O'Brien house that night to tell Mrs. O'Brien what had happened, John was awake, listening. The memory would never leave him. Ed Munro, a King County Democratic leader during much of O'Brien's political career, thought that his father's death "influenced all his later life."

One could make what one wished of the incident. A *Seattle Post-Intelligencer* editorial two days after the killing, in a tone that prefigured arguments about lenient courts a half-century later, said that James O'Brien and the two patrolmen were "all shot down by a murderous crook of the type that all the forces of sentimentalism have been put forward to protect. . . . What justification can be offered for the dereliction of courts and juries, the laxity of the parole wardens, the lubrication of all prison exits by the milk of human kindness?" The young John O'Brien did not absorb that point of view; however else the incident marked him, it did not make him a law-and-order political conservative.

On Tuesday, January 25, a funeral service was held in Saint Edward's Church, in O'Brien's neighborhood. The pallbearers included the mayor and the chief of police. The funeral cortege through downtown Seattle was a half-mile long. The police band and a squad of motorcycle patrolmen led the cortege as it moved down Yesler Street, up Second Avenue, up Olive Street, and along Seventh. People jammed the sidewalks. "By the size of the throngs that lined the streets," a paper said, "it seemed that all Seattle had turned out." John would remember the sense of public ceremony and significance, as well as the loss.

A few days earlier, the *Seattle Post-Intelligencer* had said that James O'Brien's "widow and four children were wondering what they would do; they have no savings, they needed his income to live." The pension of a policeman's widow kept them out of poverty, but close enough to it, O'Brien said later, to give him a natural sympathy for the have-nots.

John O'Brien was the oldest of the four children. The summer he was eleven, his strong-willed mother sent him to work in a grocery around the corner on Orcas Street. The store was owned by an Irish-American friend of the family named Keefe. O'Brien got $3 a week. "Every week, I'd ask Keefe for a raise, and he'd tell me that's all he could afford to pay. I worked there part-time all through high school."

O'Brien went to Catholic elementary and high schools,

St. Edward's and O'Dea. The church permeated neighborhood and family life. "St. Edward's Church was just around the corner," he recalled, "so we were very close to the church and the school and the priests and the nuns." His first job, as a young boy, was cutting grass and cleaning up at the church. And his first exposure to politics came through his mother's involvement in the church. She was well known in her parish and her community. Her house was often full of people. She was never active in party politics, but "people running for public office always wanted to see my mother," O'Brien recalled. They wanted to capitalize on her stature in the community. They wanted her to stand outside the polls and hand out their literature. The lesson may have been that she was important because of who she was, not because of her stands on the issues.

O'Brien first got interested in politics in 1928, when another Irish Catholic, Al Smith, ran for president. It seemed natural for an Irish kid to be a Democrat, anyway. O'Brien was in high school. He did not get involved in the campaign, but he did argue with the backers of Herbert Hoover.

He first did more than argue about politics six years later, when he helped Jack Taylor, a progressive Catholic Democrat from the neighborhood, get elected King County commissioner. Taylor was only five years older than O'Brien. He, too, had gone to St. Edward's School. He ran a grocery business nearby. "I had a car, and I used to drive him around," O'Brien recalled. "And I'd pass out literature." The effort paid off. Taylor won, and O'Brien was launched on a lifetime in politics.

In 1938, Taylor and other friends urged O'Brien to run for the House. He ran, but the state senate sounded better to him than the House, so he tried for a vacant senate seat. Another candidate in the Democratic primary for that senate seat was Albert Rosellini. A third, O'Brien recalled, "was another Irishman named Callahan who lived on the same street as me, across Rainier Avenue. So Rosellini won. We split the Irish vote pretty good. But in addition, Rosellini was well organized, far more than I was at that time." O'Brien finished second. He would never again run for anything but the House. Taylor and his other friends told him not to worry—he'd win the next time.

The next time, after filling Harry Austin's vacant seat, was 1940. O'Brien ran for the House, and, just as his friends had assured him, he did win the Democratic primary. In the general election, he was on the ticket with Rosellini, not against him. He also shared the ballot with statewide Initiatives 139 and 141. A lot of his political future was on that ballot. Not only was Rosellini to be governor during most of the years he served as Speaker; the issues raised by the initiatives would occupy the legislature for much of the next quarter century. Initiative 141, pushed by the radical Washington Old-Age Pension Union, would guarantee every old-age pensioner a minimum of $40 a month. The federal government was not picking up much of the tab for the elderly yet, and pensions were a real concern. In 1940, some 39,000 people in Washington were getting pensions that averaged $22.14 a month. The Pension Union, led by state legislators William Pennock and Thomas Rabbitt, wanted to nearly double that figure at one stroke, getting an additional $9 each from the federal government and the state. Pennock and Rabbitt were known as radicals, but the Pension Union had a lot of grassroots support. If the Pension Union's initiative passed, its financial impact would clearly be enormous. It won by a margin of three to two. The day after the election, the *Seattle Times* suggested that the "effects of Initiative 141 on the people of the state loom as more far-reaching than of any other on the ballot." The *Times* was probably right. The initiative began decades of conflict between progressive social legislation and a regressive revenue system. How to pay for the pension would be the most pressing question of O'Brien's first legislative term. Paying for a subsequent initiative would challenge the legislature in the years leading up to his Speakership.

The other initiative on the 1940 ballot, 139, was the first of many attempts to limit the powers of public utility districts. Public power was a big issue in rural areas, where people still lived in pre-industrial conditions without electricity—no electric lights, water pumps, milking machines, kitchen ranges, washing machines—because private power companies were not eager to string transmission lines many miles to few homes. The price of power was a consideration, too, as was the fact that Washington's private utilities were owned by Eastern holding companies. Local owners might have been less insensitive to local feelings. In 1928, the Washington Grange, with its strength in agricultural eastern Washington, had persuaded the public to pass an initiative to the legislature permitting the formation of public utility districts (PUDs). The private companies had a lot of influence in Olympia, though, and the 1929 session of the legislature refused to pass the Grange initiative. That sent it automatically to the people, who passed it in 1930.

Passage of the law and the formation of PUDs did not end the controversy. New PUDs did not appear in a vacuum. Private utilities were already there. Public power could spread only at the expense of private—which it was more than willing to do. The right of PUDs to condemn private utility property became the focus of political warfare that continued, in one form or another, for more than thirty years.

Public power was a natural Democratic issue. It provided both a perfect opportunity to champion the little guy against big business and a perfect constituency for the New Deal. It was a populist cause that came to rely heavily on big government. The Washington PUDs came to depend on the power generated by federal dams on the Columbia River and the federal law that gave them first crack at that power. The federal dam system made it possible for public utilities in small communities to offer plenty of power at rock-bottom rates. It also tied the public power movement inextricably to New Deal politics.

Public power became an article of faith for rural eastern Washington Democrats. O'Brien himself had had no contact with the PUD crusade and had no particular knowledge of or interest in public power issues. But he was a New Deal Democrat, and once he entered politics at the state level, he would support public power as a matter of course. At first, he did little more than vote for the PUDs. Later, as a leader of the House Democrats, he became an advocate of public power, a champion of public power, a martyr to its cause.

But in 1940, he had nothing to say on the issue. As a candidate in an urban neighborhood, no one expected him to. Statewide candidates talked about it, though. And Senator Homer T. Bone, who was not running for anything that year, attacked the Let the People Vote League, which sponsored Initiative 139, by pointing out that nearly all its money came from private power.

The initiative would have forbidden a PUD to issue

bonds without a vote of the people. It was couched in terms of the people's right to choose, but it was seen as an attempt to hamstring the PUDs by putting their vital functions at the mercy of elections that could be controlled by the wealth and manpower of their arch rivals, the private utilities.

Initiative 139 was defeated, with people in rural areas voting heavily against it. Arthur Langlie won the governorship in a squeaker, with absentee ballots deciding the outcome. O'Brien's old friend, Jack Taylor, was elected state land commissioner.

In the 33rd District, as expected, all three Democrats won handily. O'Brien led the voting for the House of Representatives with 9,366. Armstrong followed with 8,842. Their Republican opponents straggled in with 5,657 and 5,312 votes.

John O'Brien was in the legislature—or would be, when the session began in January. The legislative politicking started even before he reached Olympia. Ed Reilly, a Spokane lawyer who had been a star football tackle at Gonzaga, wanted to break tradition by becoming Speaker of the House a second time, and when he was in Seattle, he talked with O'Brien to enlist his support. The attention was flattering. "I sort of admired his personality," O'Brien said years later, "the way he could make you feel so important." It was not simple flattery. Reilly told O'Brien he would let him second the nomination for Speaker (unusual notoriety for a freshman representative on the first day of the session), be a Democratic floor leader, and serve on the powerful Rules Committee.

Backing the right Speaker candidate was critical for a young legislator. Julia Butler Hansen, who was first elected to the House in 1938 and who became a close friend and ally of O'Brien, recalled that "it was all wheeling and dealing when I went [to Olympia.] You had two elections: You were elected to your seat; then you had to support the right Speaker or you didn't get on the right committees."

When O'Brien drove off in his DeSoto to Olympia, sixty miles south of Seattle, he expected to be more than a face in the crowd. A 1941 photograph shows a confident man in rimless glasses, dressed for success in a wide striped tie and pin-striped suit. In Olympia, he put himself right at the social center of things.

Olympia was very much a provincial capital, with some 13,000 people, fifteen lumber, plywood, shingle, and furniture mills, and ten dairy and poultry processing plants. Dial telephones had arrived in 1938, but streets were still paved with brick. The first state capitol, which resembled a New England town hall with its cupola and widow's walk, its railed porch and balcony, its white picket fence out front, had been replaced at the turn of the century. But the newest capitol, with its impressive dome, bronze doors, and imported marble, had been completed only thirteen years before. The town's center of gravity remained north of the new dome, where the turreted stone walls of the previous capitol still loomed over the east side of Sylvester Park. On the south side of the park stood the bus depot, with its curving metal Art Deco canopy out front. On the north side, right by the old capitol, stood the brick Olympian Hotel, the deep bays of its tall, arched dining room windows facing the park.

The Olympian was the city's social center. The lobbyists and most of the legislators who counted held court in its dining rooms and lobby. A person could sit in the lobby and think nothing had changed for decades. Senator P. H. Carlyon, who had served at the turn of the century, was there chatting with old pals. The former chief clerk of the House, Charles Maybury, was holding forth there, too.

Olympia was ill-equipped to handle the extra 1,000 people who descended on it when the legislature met. Housing was tight. Army officers and their families from Fort Lewis and Camp Murray had taken some of the choicer houses and rooms. A frugal legislator could still find a room in a private home for $15 a month—but only if he did not mind a substantial walk to the capitol. A good hotel room with a bath would set him back $3.50 a night—and it might be hard to come by. Hotels were trying to talk permanent guests into taking smaller rooms, so they could accommodate more legislators and hangers-on.

Most legislators boarded in private homes. A distinct minority lived in hotels. A very small minority lived at the Olympian. O'Brien got himself a room at the Olympian right away. "It was the place to stay," he explained later. "I had no desire to stay in somebody's house."

The system O'Brien found in Olympia dumped many a legislator into the lap of the not-unwilling lobbyist. A legislator got $5 a day while the legislature was in session. Even in 1941, that was not an extravagant sum. Some legislators routinely relied on lobbyists to buy them dinner and do other favors. "That's when the boys were out hunting for what the boys called, quote, 'the pigeons,'" Julia Butler Hansen recalled. Even when the per diem rose slightly, many legislators kept a sharp eye peeled. "When I was chairman of the Highways Committee," she said (she was made chairman in 1949), "members would come to me and say, 'Find me a pigeon.'"

There were plenty of pigeons. A legislator who ran a small business or a farm back home could go to Olympia and find himself surrounded by people eager to do him favors. As Ed Reilly used to say—in a phrase that O'Brien never forgot—"For sixty days you're a king; then the medals come off."

Some members made the most of those sixty days. Hansen once heard another member ask Army Armstrong why he ran for office. Armstrong replied: "For the green stuff, boy; for the green stuff."

O'Brien stood above, or at least apart from, this seamy, grasping side of the legislature. "He wasn't a schemer," Hansen said. "I never felt he was what we used to call 'a bag man.' "

Ed Reilly turned out to have spoken too soon about giving O'Brien a seat on the Rules Committee. O'Brien got seats on Banks and Banking, Claims and Auditing, Insurance, Memorials, even Roads and Bridges, but not on Rules. His fellow 33rd District Democrat, Army Armstrong, chaired Rules, and he objected to having a freshman legislator on the committee. O'Brien sat in on the committee's first meeting, but that was all. After the meeting, Reilly took him out into the hallway and said he was sorry, but a seat on Rules was one promise he would not be able to keep.

O'Brien did, however, get to give a seconding speech. It was his first speech in the House. He was impressed by all the marble and by the size of the room: "It was about the biggest thing I'd ever seen." Someone told him to focus his eyes back on the corner of the south gallery, so he would not have to notice the stares of the other legislators or the size of the room. That was what he did.

He soon got used to speaking under the big chandeliers, surrounded by marble. From his seat in the front row beside Army Armstrong (O'Brien's conservative

Democratic predecessor had refused to sit with Armstrong), Reilly let him make a lot of the routine procedural motions. It was O'Brien who moved every morning to dispense with the reading of the journal. It was O'Brien who moved, whenever necessary, to suspend the rules of the House.

This was humdrum stuff, but it kept the legislative wheels turning. O'Brien was involved less in the mechanics of passing individual bills than of running the House. Presiding would become his area of expertise, and it would remain his focus in the years to come.

"The days were long and arduous," O'Brien recalled years later. "You had oral roll calls. You'd be working on the floor of the House until two or three o'clock in the morning with endless roll calls." The tedium was broken by intensely partisan skirmishes. "You had more partisan efforts in the early days," O'Brien said. During the 1940s, "there was a tendency to demand the previous question and cut off people, to allow only two or three speeches on each side and then stop it." Legislators did not always confine themselves to parliamentary niceties. "I remember George Hurley [a Seattle Democrat far to the left of Reilly] in my first session getting up and standing on top of his desk and yelling at the Speaker."

The overall tone, though, was not one of anarchy—to the contrary. "We had great formality then," O'Brien said, "because we had a chief clerk who had been there for years, Si Holcomb, who revered the Speaker's rostrum."

O'Brien got to watch the man on the rostrum at close range. He saw that Ed Reilly talked with both Democratic and Republican leaders every morning, so that there would be no surprises. In fact, the freshman got to join Armstrong and other senior legislators in the Speaker's office for those sessions. He also saw the way Reilly maneuvered on the rostrum. Reilly was "a master of delaying," using parliamentary maneuvers and sometimes just walking out. He always buttressed his position with precedents, however inappropriate they might turn out to be. "He always wanted to talk about precedents," O'Brien recalled. "There are some *Mason's Precedents and Parliamentary Procedures* books we have in the back of the chamber that go back to 1848 or 1850. Reilly would like to talk about the precedents established in *Mason's.*" If O'Brien looked closely at one of the precedents Reilly cited, though, "it wouldn't mean a thing."

Reilly was much too conservative for the left-wing Democrats in the House. A divided Democratic majority was nothing new. Charles Hodde, who was elected to the House in 1937, recalled nearly a half century later that in the 1937 legislature—when Reilly was Speaker for the first time—"we had an organization [in the House] of three caucuses . . . We had a right-wing caucus and a left-wing caucus. There were sixteen of us in what we called the wishbone caucus, all Democrats, but we wouldn't caucus with the left-wing Democrats nor with the right wing, which included the Republicans with the more conservative Democrats." The wishbone caucus was gone by 1941, but Reilly ran the House with a coalition of conservative Democrats and Republicans. O'Brien threw in his lot with his party's conservative wing.

The 1941 legislature opened at a time of conflict and limited optimism. Two weeks earlier, papers had noted that there seemed to be fewer people than usual in the streets of Seattle on New Year's Eve. One could hardly blame anybody who had second thoughts about celebrating. A British spokesman kicked off the new year by announcing that Hitler would probably invade in March. The Germans were bombing London. Roosevelt, in his State of the Union Address, outlined the lend-lease program and asked for unlimited aid to Britain.

In Washington, where the effects of the Depression had been especially severe—the 1940 census revealed that Seattle had slipped from twentieth- to twenty-second-largest American city—expansion of the war meant primarily a promise of economic growth. The Seattle-Tacoma Shipbuilding Company said in early January that it planned a $2-million expansion of its Tacoma plant if the company got a contract for two 35,000-ton passenger ships that could be converted to carriers. Congressman Warren Magnuson, who seemed to make almost daily announcements of federal largesse, said the contract would be forthcoming. Magnuson was well launched on his long career of bringing home the bacon.

Thanks to the growing military demand for aluminum—and the power from the brand-new federal dams on the Columbia River—the aluminum industry was building its first plants in Washington. Aluminum, shipbuilding, and other wartime industries attracted workers from all over. The local population booms they created were a mixed blessing. School districts in areas with a lot of defense work, forced to accommodate more students almost overnight, had trouble coming up with the money to build new schools.

Most of the economic headlines, though, were not about the developing wartime boom; they were about lingering Depression-era conflicts. A lumber strike had been settled just the month before. Later in January, a national defense commissioner policing costs for defense supplies warned that unless the lumber industry immediately cut its prices to "a decent level," he would recommend that lumber be drafted "the way we draft men." The National Labor Relations Board held hearings in Tacoma to decide whether the AFL or the CIO had bargaining rights in Puget Sound ports.

The legislature started right off with a battle of its own. The Speaker having been elected and other internal business put out of the way, the Democrats started the session by trying to prevent the seating of Governor-elect Arthur Langlie. It was the act of politicians secure in their insularity, unashamed of parochialism. The official balloting had been close: 392,522 for Langlie; 386,706 for Dill. Democratic partisans in both Olympia and Seattle had already filed protests about crossover voting: ballots were still marked by hand, and a number of voters had checked the top of the Democratic column, indicating a preference for the Democratic party, then had crossed over to the Republican column to single out Langlie. The instructions on the ballot said this was legal, and it had been declared legal by the incumbent attorney general, but it was challenged anyway. The Democratic Central Committee pushed the challenge. State Democratic Chairman Clarence Coleman had formally notified Langlie that his election would be contested before the legislature.

On the second day of the session, after hotel-room strategy sessions that lasted until 3:00 A.M., the Democrats dropped everything to caucus about Langlie. The House and senate were meeting together. After the caucus, Albert Rosellini moved to investigate the vote count. Both Rosellini and Armstrong from the 33rd District voted for the motion. O'Brien joined the Speaker in voting against it. The audience applauded as the motion was defeated, 97 to 45. When Lieutenant Governor Victor A. Meyers finally signed Langlie's certificate of election, spectators clapped and cheered.

With Langlie installed as governor, the legislature started out by doing very little. The senate wrangled over internal issues, and not much work was done. The war was very much on people's minds—the fighting for North Africa and the bombing of Britain and Germany were constantly in the news—and while issues of war and peace obviously fell far outside the legislature's sphere of authority, that did not prevent legislators from putting in their own two cents. Early in the session, the left-wing Democrats introduced a resolution criticizing Roosevelt for helping the British, and the conservative Democrats introduced a resolution praising him. A group of "women for peace" showed up in the gallery holding antiwar signs. When Army Armstrong shouted "Aye!" to the resolution praising Roosevelt, the women started chanting "We want peace!" Reilly banged the gavel, but could not make them stop; eventually, he had the sergeant at arms evict them. The House voted 76 to 20 to commend Roosevelt. When it voted against the resolution criticizing him, the white-haired Reverend Edward Pettus shouted, "This is a war for economic empire!"

The war stirred passions, but the real issue in Olympia was money. Pocket money was of some concern, as Reilly cut the salaries of House employees while legislators voted themselves another $5 a day in expense money. But the big concern was the state budget, already $7 million in the red and likely to be stretched even thinner by the $40-a-month pension law. The pension was far and away the largest drain on state finances. Langlie estimated at first that it would cost $42.8 million. Part way through the session he increased the estimate to $54 million. The whole state budget amounted to only $220 million. And that was a record.

Perhaps inevitably, given the factionalism of the time, the legislature's fight to pay for the pension initiative led to a fight over keeping tabs on—or harassing—the people who had won its passage. On March 6—the day before Seattle was to experiment with its first wartime blackout—the House considered a bill that would have required any organization supported by people on old-age assistance or relief to report any contribution over one dollar. Two Seattle legislators, William Pennock and Richard A. Murphy, led the fight against the bill. Pennock, in addition to being secretary of the Pension Union, was also a leader of the radical Democrats in the House.

The pension forces filibustered for hours, showering the bill with amendments, demanding time-consuming roll call votes. They finally wore down their opponents. The House voted to send the bill back to the Rules Committee. O'Brien got his first look at the power of the filibuster.

No one knew exactly how the pensions would be financed. The Pension Union had deliberately left vague the source of funding. During the campaign, some of its backers had explained that "four years ago, a pension initiative was defeated because the people, although favoring the pension increase, nevertheless disapproved of the specific tax." They did not repeat that mistake. Unofficially, they did talk about a new tax on stocks, bonds, mortgages, and other "intangibles." They claimed it would tap the "56 percent of Washington wealth now untaxed." There was no precedent for a tax on intangibles, though, and there was no precedent for imposing one. Washington was, by and large, stuck with the tax system it already had.

Until the Depression, the state had relied almost entirely on a property tax. Then, after the economy crashed, farmers in particular found themselves with lots of land and no cash to pay the taxes on it. The Grange consequently sponsored an initiative to give the state an income tax. The initiative passed in 1932, but the state supreme court soon declared it unconstitutional.

The voters not only approved an income tax in 1932; they also imposed a 40-mill limit on property taxes. To plug the resulting gap in state revenues until the income tax went into effect, the 1933 legislature imposed a business and occupation tax—taxing the total amount a business took in, whether it was making a profit or taking a loss. Then, after the income tax was thrown out and it became clear that the revenue gap would be permanent, the 1935 legislature imposed a tax on retail sales. Some store owners protested that, in the depths of the Depression, they could not pass along an extra charge to their customers, but their protests fell on deaf ears. Sales taxes are often considered regressive because they do not explicitly force rich people to pay more than poor. This one seemed less regressive than it might have because it did not tax the necessities of life: purchases of bread, milk, butter, eggs, and produce were exempt. Those exemptions did not last. The state's need for money soon overcame any legislative scruples about taxing food. Pressed for funds, the 1939 legislature extended the sales tax to groceries.

Now, pressed even harder, the 1941 legislature had to decide how much further it wanted to go. The idea of an income tax was still very much in the air. Two weeks into the session, the state's tax commissioner, T. M. Jenner, warned members of the House Revenue Committee against making any drastic change in the state's revenue structure. Setting a pattern that would be repeated more than forty years later, state officials were trying to use tax policy as a means of attracting new industry. "There is a tax race on between Oregon and Washington to attract new industries," Jenner said. He told the committee that Washington had gotten the Aluminum Corporation of America not merely because its taxes were lower than Oregon's but also because the system seemed more stable. "The first investigation the aluminum company made when it thought of locating in this area concerned the tax structure of the two states," he said.

A radical revision of the tax structure certainly was not the only means legislators considered for increasing revenue. But most of the alternatives would not have raised enough money—and they did not pass, anyway. A resolution that called for the establishment of a state lottery was voted down in the senate. A tax on chain stores was pushed vigorously but unsuccessfully in the House by Hugh D. Rosellini, Albert Rosellini's Tacoma cousin. At Ed Reilly's request, John O'Brien introduced a bill that would have placed a specific tax on bowling alleys. Bowling was becoming popular; taxing it would have provided at least one more drop in the bucket. Bowling alley owners descended on Olympia to protest. The bill failed.

The little specialized taxes were a diversion. The state's revenue problem gave the legislators a political choice that was difficult but clear: they could persuade voters to pass a constitutional amendment permitting a graduated income tax, or they could increase the sales tax. Those remained the basic choices for John O'Brien's next forty-eight years in Olympia. Then, as later, the sales tax was the surer thing. But in 1941, raising the sales tax was not something to be undertaken lightly. The original statute had set the tax at 2 percent, and that had become a magic number. One might tamper with the tax a little—for instance, by applying it to food—but adding to that 2 percent would be a big step.

On February 19—two days after having voted against the sale of beer on Saturday nights, and after having approved immediate reconstruction of the Tacoma Narrows Bridge (which had collapsed the year before, just five months after it had opened)—the House voted 76 to 16 for a referendum on the income tax. O'Brien voted with the majority.

Eight days later, Governor Langlie proposed boosting the sales tax to 3 percent. On March 7, O'Brien joined the majority in voting for the tax increase, pending a constitutional amendment to permit an income tax as well. It was a controversial decision. The Grange promptly threatened a referendum on the sales tax increase. The Taxpayers Union proposed limiting the tax increase to one biennium, and letting the people vote on an income tax. The House soon passed a constitutional amendment that could be submitted to the voters at the next general election. But that all proved academic. No income tax was passed. The real milestone was breaking the 2-percent barrier on the sales tax.

The die was cast for future increases. Forced to choose between raising the sales tax and limiting the growth of government, the legislature would vote tax increases time and again. Tax reform was to prove a chimera. It was a chimera that O'Brien often chased. He continued to believe that a graduated income tax was the fairest way for the state to raise money. But tax reform did not come any closer to reality as time went on. Even when the legislators voted to put an income tax amendment on the ballot in later years, the people of the state voted against it.

For O'Brien, perhaps the most interesting part of the session came at its end. Reilly had been unable to make good his promise to put O'Brien on the Rules Committee. At the end of the session, he made up for it by appointing O'Brien to serve with the governor, one other representative, two senators, and two judges on the State Charitable, Penal, and Reformatory Interim Investigating Committee studying state institutions.

The legislature met for only sixty days every two years. There was no full-time legislative staff. Legislators did not even have offices, much less staff. A committee chairman might set up shop in his committee's hearing room, but any legislator who was not a chairman had to do paperwork, meet constituents, and even dictate letters at his desk on the floor. Without a staff, the only way to get work done between sessions was through specially appointed interim committees.

The interim investigating committee visited state mental hospitals and other institutions. Some of the more barbaric practices—such as punishing reformatory girls who broke the rules by cutting off all their hair and putting them in rooms without furniture—had been stopped, but the committee found a harshly repressive environment. The visits were eye-openers for O'Brien. He saw Seattle-born movie actress Frances Farmer pushing a broom in a women's dormitory at Western State Hospital. But faded glamor seemed almost a grace note. The overall impression was stark. "It was medieval," he remembered years later. "We saw patients lying like cordwood on the floors in the lavatories. We rounded a corner, and a guard had a patient down and was beating him. It was horrible."

O'Brien came away from his first legislative session knowing that he wanted to be Speaker. He would sometimes stand at the south side of the capitol, look over at the brick walls of the governor's mansion, and think he might like to be governor some day. But he *knew* he wanted to be Speaker. He liked the House, the ceremony, the legislature as a self-contained society, "the whole surroundings, the atmosphere." Some people who had observed O'Brien during his early years in the House were surprised when he later became Speaker. He had not seemed gregarious enough; people tended to recall that "he wasn't a glad-hander." ("He really isn't much different now than he was then," says state supreme court Justice Fred Dore, a former legislator who knew O'Brien in the old neighborhood. "John has always been kind of standoffish and formal.") O'Brien did not make an early mark as a debater. But he did work hard. And he had the drive to succeed. Mort Frayn, a Republican who preceded O'Brien as Speaker, says that those who really knew O'Brien were aware of his ambition all along. They would have been surprised if he had *not* become Speaker. Julia Butler Hansen found him a "kind of relaxed" legislator, but certainly she was not surprised by his ambition to become Speaker. "Oh my no!" she laughed. O'Brien himself says today: "I was always ambitious. I always felt a desire to go all the way and become Speaker of the House. It probably started in my first session before I ever arrived in Olympia."

II

Close to Power, but Not Close Enough

O'BRIEN FIRST TRIED FOR THE SPEAKERSHIP IN 1943. It was a brash move. Not only was he challenging his old benefactor, Ed Reilly—he had no misgivings about that; he felt it was not disloyalty, just politics—but he had served only one term. He was not yet a leader. He did not seem to have a chance. In fact, he thought less about winning than about making a reputation. And yet, there was an outside chance: if the two main contenders, Reilly and Ralph L. J. Armstrong of Olympia, wound up dead-locked, O'Brien might become a compromise choice. The contest did start out deadlocked, but Reilly soon prevailed. After his nomination was made and seconded, the *Seattle Post-Intelligencer* reported, "There was a parade of further seconding speeches by representatives, including John L. O'Brien, an early contender for the Speakership." He was getting noticed—and was being taken seriously.

This was O'Brien's time for moving into the public eye. The election of 1942 had presented little difficulty. He had outdrawn not only the Republican candidates but also the veteran Army Armstrong. Rating candidates, the Mu-

31

nicipal League had described him as intelligent and experienced.

He still was not saying much about the issues. Rather, he was painting himself as a pragmatist, a New Deal Democrat who was also a hardheaded man with a dollar. The wartime economic boom had stuffed the state's coffers with sales-tax money. The financial squeeze of 1941 had turned into a surplus. Before the Municipal League rated O'Brien for the 1942 elections, he sat through an interview in which he was asked, "Would you be in favor of spending the surplus that the state has on hand?" He answered that as a certified public accountant, "figures are not foreign to me and I don't believe in squandering money. I don't believe in all these old-time politicians running wild with our tax money. If there is a definite need—spend it, but I would like to know what for first." (O'Brien later found it hard to believe that he had talked about "old-time politicians running wild.")

The war ran through everything. When the 1943 legislature opened on January 11, the Marines were fighting at Guadalcanal and the Germans were besieging Leningrad. Washington's Japanese and Japanese American residents had already been shipped off to internment camps. An estimated 50,000 women were working at defense jobs in the state.

Cities, counties, and school districts found themselves with wartime population bulges and too little money to pay for the extra services that extra people required. It was clear before the legislative session started that O'Brien and his fellow legislators would have to consider bailing out those hard-pressed local governments.

In February, O'Brien voted with all but one of his Seattle colleagues against a motion to send a $4-million aid bill for cities back to committee. The motion passed. But the next day, the urban legislators prevailed; a majority decided not to bury the bill after all. When the session was over, the executives of the Association of Washington Cities sent O'Brien a thank-you note, observing that "the municipal tax base has been broadened, and a long step toward a more permanent solution of the fiscal problem has been taken."

Bailing out the cities, crucial though it may have been, was not the big issue of the 1943 legislature. Actually, there were two big issues. One was another public power bill, Initiative 12, which the voters had sent to the legislature at the previous general election. Initiative 12 would have allowed PUDs in different counties to join forces and take over the entire system of a private power company. (Existing law permitted a public utility district to operate only within a single county. It enabled a private utility to operate in many counties. A single PUD therefore could not take over a big private system. At best, a group of PUDs could do it piecemeal, one county at a time. Leaders of the public power movement wanted the ability to take over whole systems.)

A similar bill had died in committee in 1941. Now, the question was whether to submit it to a referendum. The senate passed it narrowly on February 16. The next day, the House passed it 62 to 37, with O'Brien voting yes. The *Seattle Times* warned that passage of Initiative 12 would "sound the death knell of nearly all private power companies in the state." That would have suited the public power movement just fine, but the *Times* need not have worried. The bill passed with an emergency clause that put it into effect immediately, but the clause was struck down by the state supreme court. In 1944, the voters rejected the rest of the initiative, too. War or peace, the battles over public power went on.

The other big issue in the legislature was Governor Langlie's attempt to deal with possible enemy invasion. In retrospect that was, perhaps, a strange time for the governor to be alarmed about war coming to Washington State. Although things looked bleak at the time, the tide was clearly turning in the United States's favor. While the legislature was in session, the Russians broke the siege of Leningrad, Allied bombing drove Rommel's Afrika Korps from Tripoli, General MacArthur took New Guinea, and the United States gained control of the Solomon Islands. On the other hand, American bases in the Aleutians were bombed, and the regional civil defense director, James C. Sheppard, said that the danger of an attack on the West Coast was greater than ever. "The Pacific Coast will probably be attacked," he said in late February. "It's time we faced that threat."

Langlie faced the threat by presenting the legislature with a package of six bills requesting war powers. Some of the language was uncontroversial—the bills would have enabled the governor to survey the supplies of food and other necessities within the state, to cooperate with all federal departments, and to set up salvage and waste-prevention measures. But they would also have allowed the governor to suspend or modify any state statute that the president, his naval or military cabinet officers, or the U.S. attorney general said was impeding the war effort.

The governor's proposal immediately became a partisan issue. As O'Brien and other Democrats saw it—or chose to see it—"he was trying to become a dictator." When Langlie was mayor of Seattle, he had won over an initially hostile city council; as governor, however, he was not going to win over O'Brien and a hostile Democratic majority. The bills were referred to the House Committee on Civil Defense, on which O'Brien sat; and he led the fight against them. "I guess we didn't think the threat of invasion was all that serious," O'Brien recalled. The Democrats thought Langlie was "asking for something that wasn't warranted and wasn't needed." That being the case, "we were very reluctant to give him those strong powers."

The chairman of the committee, Francis Pearson, "was a [nearly] blind legislator who was trying to get Governor Langlie to appoint him to a war defense office of some sort," O'Brien said. Because Pearson wanted to curry Langlie's favor, "he was with the governor. We had a time with Francis trying to get the bill amended or killed. We used to tease him about it later."

O'Brien and the other partisans on the committee managed to get around Pearson. On February 8, Acting Attorney General Fred E. Lewis told the committee that five of the bills were unconstitutional. Pearson offered to meet with Lewis and Langlie in the morning to work things out. O'Brien was not about to give Pearson *carte blanche;* instead, he introduced a resolution that set up a bipartisan five-member committee to work with the governor and the attorney general to redraft the bills. His resolution passed.

The next day, O'Brien's subcommittee did meet with Lewis and the governor, but Langlie held out strongly for his own versions of the bills. Pearson wanted to oblige Langlie. After the meeting, he said he was tired of "monkeying around" with technicalities and would try to get the bills out of committee that same week. He did try, but O'Brien and O'Brien's allies on the committee were too strong for him.

Several newspapers were rooting for the governor. "Some of the snipers are taking selfish political potshots and saying that it's a terrible thing to give Langlie dictatorial powers," the *Seattle Times* editorialized. "Perhaps in this case, the military might better handle such snipers."

On February 15 O'Brien wrote to Warren Magnuson: "The Democratic members of the committee feel that the bills give to the Governor entirely too broad powers, and, also, they [are] not necessary. . . . These proposed measures of the Governor's have attracted considerable publicity, and have been favored, of course, by the press—accusing us of playing partisan politics. Tomorrow night I am speaking over the radio in behalf of our stand."

The committee struck down four of the governor's six bills, approved the attorney general's proposed substitutions for those bills, and tabled two bills that would have required the state war council to cooperate with federal agencies and would have enabled the governor to suspend the laws.

As the session drew to a close, the committee kept those two bills bottled up. The arrival of the war powers bills on the floor of the House precipitated what the *Daily Olympian* called "the worst knock-down drag-out fight of the entire Washington State legislative session." Langlie's backers tried three times to get the two bills out of committee. The votes on the bills became votes on Langlie. All three times, the governor's forces lost. O'Brien had taken on the governor and won.

A compromise was worked out just before the session ended. A war council was created—composed of the governor, the lieutenant governor, and the state insurance commissioner—with emergency powers to issue rulings with the force of law in case of invasion, air raids, floods, epidemics, bombings, the destruction of war plants or other property by sabotage or bombing, or any other war hazard to civilian lives. If this was not a great triumph for civil liberties, neither was it a headlong rush toward dictatorship. In any case, it had no practical effect.

That was the zenith—or, depending on one's perspective, the nadir—of the legislature's efforts to deal with the issues of war and peace. In retrospect, the notion of Washington bracing itself for invasion is ludicrous. Even at the time, neither side really thought invasion was imminent. Langlie thought the legislation should be in place, as a housekeeping measure, just in case. The Democrats thought even that was pretty farfetched. What might have been viewed as a matter of life or death for whole cities was treated as a narrowly partisan issue. Since the invasion never came—nor did the air raids, pestilence, or bigtime sabotage—the substance of the bills proved academic.

Nevertheless, the fight over the war powers bills put O'Brien for the first time into a position of public prominence. His first session had involved him in the mechanics of running the House. This one had put him into the spotlight.

O'Brien himself thought the war powers battle helped him most by fostering his friendship with Julia Butler Hansen, who also served on the Civilian Defense Committee. She "had a great feeling about issues on the floor: when to get involved, when not to get involved," he said. "Julia had a good sense of timing. She had that sixth sense on whether to support or oppose an issue." He was to benefit in future years from both her judgment and her support.

And his work on the House Committee on Banks and

Banking put him into the good graces of the state banking community. After the legislature adjourned, W. W. Scruby, vice-president of the Seattle First National Bank, wrote to O'Brien "as Chairman of the Legislative Committee of the Washington Bankers Association, to express to you our deep appreciation for your cooperation and efforts in securing the enactment of sound, constructive legislation presented by us. We also wish to commend you for your successful efforts in defeating some undesirable bills."

"Scruby, who lobbied for the Washington Bankers Association, had a lot of influence at that time," O'Brien said. The association itself tended to get most of what it wanted. This helped in the next session, when O'Brien chaired the Banking Committee. "I could get up on the floor of the House and say, 'This bill is sponsored by the Washington Bankers Association,' and that's all I had to say. It would fly through."

The commercial banks and the savings banks were often rivals in Olympia, but O'Brien managed to stay friendly with both camps. After the 1945 session, the president of Washington Mutual Savings Bank wrote that the bank's vice-president, Ralph R. Knapp, "has told me of the help and cooperation which you gave in securing the enactment of necessary amendments to the Mutual Savings Bank Act." The president of the United Mutual Savings Bank of Tacoma added that Knapp "has told me of the help and cooperation you so generously gave in securing the enactment of amendments which we all felt were needed."

In 1946, writing to the Municipal League, O'Brien said: "During the last session I was one of the leaders, and in that capacity helped quite considerably in the passage of many measures—particularly bills pertaining to the banking industry, and some labor bills."

As a legislator, he supported bills for both banks and organized labor, just as in private life, he did accounting for both businesses and labor groups. O'Brien always tried to keep his career as a legislator separate from his professional career. People could know him for years in Olympia without hearing anything about his businesses back home. But there were parallels.

During his early years in Olympia, bankers were not the only people who expressed their appreciation. After the 1949 session, teachers' union official Clayton Farrington noted that O'Brien had voted for a teachers' tenure law—which did not pass—and that "he has a 100-percent record all the way down the line."

Perhaps because O'Brien's father had been a detective, he took a conspicuous interest in bills that affected police and fire fighters' unions. The first major reform of the police pension laws in half a century took place while he was Speaker. Part of the new law increased benefits to widows of policemen killed in the line of duty. The lobbyist for the bill told legislators it was a bill to help John O'Brien's mother. O'Brien did not find out until later about the lobbyist's ploy. In 1948, when O'Brien was campaigning for the legislature, he wrote to the secretary of Firemen's Union Local 27: "I have always supported bills sponsored by the firemen's unions." O'Brien noted in the same letter that for the past five years, he had been auditor and accountant for Aeronautical Industry District Lodge 751, the Boeing workers' big blue-collar union.

O'Brien got reelected with little effort in 1944, piling up more votes than any other legislative candidate in the city. He got 4 percent more votes than his Democratic running mate, Army Armstrong, and 83 percent more than the nearest Republican. It was a good year for Democrats. Franklin Delano Roosevelt won his fourth term as president. In Washington State, the popular New Deal Democratic senator, Mon Wallgren, defeated Langlie for governor. And radical Hugh B. DeLacy, a former University of Washington English instructor who had been elected to the Seattle City Council as a candidate of the Washington Commonwealth Federation and whom some people considered an out-and-out communist, won a seat in Congress.

Once again, O'Brien took a shot at getting elected Speaker. Shortly after the election, he started lining up allies. On November 20, he wrote to Robert F. Waldron of Spokane, a former Speaker who was just returning to the House, asking for his support and expressing "the belief that I have the ability and the necessary experience to carry out the duties of the office."

It was still too soon. The Democrats went for a lot more experience than O'Brien could offer. They chose a Thurston County legislator named George Yantis, who had been Speaker back in the turbulent session of 1933. A tall, spare man whose grandfather had been Washington Territory's first Speaker of the House, Yantis had been primarily responsible for drafting the income tax initiative of 1932. He was attractive to the conservative and middle-of-the-road legislators whose top priority was keeping the Speakership from radical Army Armstrong. Washington's drinking laws were clearly going to be fought over in Olympia, and Yantis was known as a "dry." Armstrong was described as an "ultra-wet."

O'Brien helped throw the election to Yantis. As a reward, he finally got his seat on the Rules Committee. There was no longer a conflict with Armstrong; Yantis booted his principal rival off the committee. Getting ahead in the House required getting close to the Speaker. O'Brien got very close. The new Speaker was widely respected, but he had been away from the legislature for years. O'Brien quickly made himself useful to Yantis by helping him get the lay of the land. He also put himself in a position to stand in for Yantis as spokesman for the House.

"George Yantis and Governor Wallgren didn't see eye to eye," O'Brien recalled. "Yantis had run against him or something. The Speaker never went down" to the governor's office. To keep in touch with the legislature, Wallgren talked to O'Brien and Robert Waldron. "Practically every day at five o'clock we were down at the governor's office talking to the governor about his bills," O'Brien said. He might not be Speaker, but he did get to interpret the Democratic executive and the Democratic legislature to each other.

And he did get to try running the House. "I sat right down front with Yantis," O'Brien recalled, "and occasionally, he'd let me preside." In addition, as he would write three years later in a letter to the Municipal League, "on many occasions, in the absence of the Speaker, I was the presiding officer of the House."

The war was still on. The Battle of the Bulge was in progress when the legislators assembled in January 1945. While they were in Olympia, the U.S. Marines took Iwo Jima and the Russians reached Berlin. When the federal government decided it was all right to bring at least some of the interned Japanese Americans back to the Pacific Coast, the state's new governor would have none of it. "You'd think the war was all over and our boys halfway home," Wallgren said. "The vast majority of them undoubtedly are all right, but there is no one who can guarantee the loyalty and conduct of them all."

The wartime boom had wiped out the state's deficit. Instead of red ink, legislators found themselves with a lot of wartime tax revenues and a lot of ideas about how to spend them when the fighting stopped. The labor lobby was the strongest it had ever been. The old-age pensions that had been a source of financial worry in the 1941 session had entered Democratic orthodoxy. O'Brien was part of a Democratic program committee that recommended, as the session began, that old-age pensions increase with the cost of living.

A $40 minimum pension had been a controversial issue five years before. This time, a bill to increase the minimum pension to $50 was passed without a dissenting vote in either house. Contemplating a surplus of more than $70 million, the 1945 legislature may have been the most fiscally liberal in the state's history. It had plenty of encouragement to spend—pressure groups were well aware of the surplus—and, since virtually no expenditure would require an immediate tax increase, it had little reason to be frugal.

A politician not eager to spend could make himself unpopular in a hurry. Governor Wallgren's veto of a teachers' pension bill soon cost him support. He opposed the bill on the grounds that it benefited other public school employees, as well as teachers. O'Brien voted for it.

Wallgren's attempts to dominate state boards and commissions cost him even more support. Sportsmen had worked hard to establish an independent game commission. Wallgren wanted the power to appoint and fire game commissioners at will. He got the legislature to place a referendum giving him that power on the 1946 general election ballot, but when 1946 rolled around, the referendum was rejected overwhelmingly. In the meantime, Wallgren's attempt to run the game commission earned him a lot of animosity.

Wallgren also wanted to establish a timber resources board that would effectively give him control over state-owned timber. Since the revenue from state timber sales went to the public schools, the PTA was more than a little concerned. State Superintendent of Public Instruction Pearl Wanamaker said Wallgren's attempt to get his hands on the timber was "all part of a plot to obtain complete domination of the state." The proposed timber resources board was also rejected by the people.

O'Brien, who had to explain the governor's proposals to the legislature, felt that Wallgren "wanted to be another Huey Long." Other people figured the governor could be and had been bought by special interests. Whatever his motivation, the popular senator quickly transformed himself into a governor who could not win a second term.

While Wallgren was trying to extend his political reach, the legislators were trying to make personal ends meet. The legislature's personal financial concerns cast it in a light of threadbareness and petty venality. Before the session even started, the papers reported that legislators would vote on a bill to increase their subsistence allowance from $5 to $10 a day. Eating costs in Olympia were at least $3 to $4.50 a day, and the rent for a room in a private house had risen during the war, from $18 to $30 a month to $12 to $25 a week. Some legislators were making the best of their otherwise pinched service in the state capital. At least thirty-five wives of House members were on the House payroll.

The big issue of the day was liquor. Prohibition had been repealed a dozen years before, but Washington law still did not permit the sale of liquor by the drink. Wallgren made a big pitch for changing the law. As a Democratic floor leader, O'Brien was to find the governor's liquor legislation his hardest sell.

In Wallgren's first address to the legislature, he argued that by making people buy liquor by the bottle or not at all, Washington was creating a state full of drunks. "Forcing people to buy liquor by the bottle [has] caused us to rank among the top five states as consuming the most liquor per capita in the whole country," he said. "As a result, we have much drunkenness. We find bottle drinking in hotels, cars, doorways, and alleys. Because they are forced to do so, people surreptitiously carry their bottles with them, as they did in Prohibition days."

Wallgren also argued that the states with which Washington was competing for tourists all offered liquor by the drink, and by not following suit, Washington was putting itself at a competitive disadvantage. "This state can and should be one of the greatest playgrounds for vacationists in the nation," he told the legislators. "To fully accomplish this, we must offer our guests all the hospitality possible."

The bill that Wallgren introduced at the end of January was more moderate than had been expected. Liberals promptly attacked it as insufficient. Drys attacked it on the ground that any tampering with the Steele Act, which had governed liquor sales since 1935, was unsound. The gist of the bill was that if local populations approved it by referendum, incorporated cities and towns could permit sales of liquor by the drink at hotels, restaurants, and clubs in downtown business districts.

The next day, the fighting started. As a member of the Committee on Liquor Control, O'Brien was in the thick of it, standing up for the governor's proposal. When the committee's chairman, Army Armstrong, said Wallgren's bill would be gutted in committee, O'Brien announced that Wallgren's supporters were organizing to report the bill out intact. "We owe it to the governor," he said, "to let the legislature vote on his measure without messing it up with demands being made by the restaurant and hotel men."

Three weeks later, the House voted down an amendment that would have put a liquor-by-the-drink referendum before the people at a special election. It was a clear vote against Wallgren. O'Brien, still taking the governor's part, tried an amendment that would have placed a referendum on the general election ballot in 1946. Wallgren's forces gained only two votes. It was hopeless. Democrats were split on the issue. Republicans were solidly against it. O'Brien could not maneuver around the basic arithmetic. The votes just were not there. Wallgren got almost everything he wanted from the 1945 legislature, but he did not get liquor by the drink.

The legislature was not reluctant to break new ground. Buoyed by plenty of money and looking forward to the end of the war, it started edging into areas where the state had never trod. In the wake of a tank-car oil spill that nearly wiped out the Soos Creek fish hatchery, and faced with recurrent worries about drinking-water supplies, the legislature passed the first water pollution control law in Washington history. O'Brien joined virtually all his colleagues in voting yes. The pollution control law had little impact at the time, but it laid a foundation for more ambitious legislation, and its language, strictly construed, was to prove crucial nearly forty years later in a debate over building hundreds of millions of dollars worth of new sewage treatment plants. The act established a state Pollution Control Commission. The commission's first chairman was O'Brien's old friend Jack Taylor, who was between terms as state land commissioner.

O'Brien served on a committee recommending that the state take over two ferry runs: between Bellingham and the San Juan Islands, and between downtown Tacoma and Fox Island. That proved the first step toward state operation of all the ferries on Puget Sound.

Probably remembering his own stint on the interim committee that investigated state institutions in 1942, O'Brien also lent his support to a suggestion that the legislature take another look. When L. R. Anderson introduced a resolution that urged the state to investigate the overcrowding of handicapped children at the Western Washington Custodial School at Buckley and the Eastern Washington Custodial School at Medical Lake, O'Brien spoke in support. The resolution passed.

O'Brien tried to do something for children in schools closer to home, too. He introduced a bill that would allow parochial school students to ride public school buses. He had been told about children trudging to parochial schools in the rain and snow while partly empty public school buses whizzed past. Now O'Brien used that image to reach his colleagues' emotions: "I was talking about the kids watching the buses go by in the rain and the snow, and I looked up at one of the legislators from Spokane, and first thing

I knew he was crying." Both houses were moved enough to pass the bill, but O'Brien's victory proved short-lived. The new law was challenged by Superintendent of Public Instruction Pearl Wanamaker, and in 1948, it was declared unconstitutional by the state supreme court. For the time being it stood, though, and it was one of the legislative accomplishments that O'Brien advertised in his next primary campaign in the heavily Catholic 33rd District.

When O'Brien went to the voters in the summer of 1946, the war had ended, the servicemen were coming home, and the wartime economic boom was over. The state, like the nation, was on the verge of new things. O'Brien himself seemed on the verge of new political success. He was a floor leader and the press had started to notice him. He had a solidly Democratic district. He was on good terms with the governor.

Back home in the district, he was much in evidence. As chairman of the Rainier Businessmen's Club's street lighting committee, he was pressuring the Seattle City Council and the mayor to get traffic signals and street lights on Rainier Avenue and Empire Way. The committee had petitions in almost all the stores in the district. O'Brien had been president of the Businessmen's Club, and he was already being referred to as the "perennial chairman" of the Rainier District Pow Wow.

His platform for the 1946 primary reflected the state's wartime sense of prosperity. It included a "financially sound Teachers' Retirement Law; adequate old-age pensions; adequate basic state school support; greater distribution of state tax revenue to the City of Seattle; a soldiers' bonus and other assistance to the veterans; general protection of labor and the small businessman; state aid for re-

lief of the housing shortage; development of our
Washington resources; encouragement of more industries for more jobs."

Those were standard Democratic goals. But the election
of 1946, in Washington and in the United States as a whole,
was not shaping up as a standard Democratic election.
Franklin D. Roosevelt was gone. There was fighting in
China, violence in Palestine, and a whole gamut of labor
conflicts at home. The postwar wave of anticommunist
hysteria was rising. The Republicans were ready for a
comeback.

In Washington, the Republicans were running against
radicalism, both real and perceived. The campaign to drive
Hugh DeLacy out of Congress received the most press,
but other races also had an ideological tone. A former
state commander of the American Legion, Homer Jones,
was running against DeLacy, alleging communist influence in the Democratic party. Harry Cain, a former mayor
of Tacoma, was making similar charges in his race for
Wallgren's vacant senate seat. State legislators William
Pennock and Thomas Rabbitt, and the executive secretary
of the Democratic State Central Committee, Jerry O'Con-
nell, were also being attacked as Reds.

In O'Brien's own district, where left-wing sentiments
remained fairly strong and there was a host of Democratic
candidates, the main controversy centered on Senator Albert Rosellini. Opponents claimed he was using his political position for the benefit of his law firm. A community
newspaper editorialized against him for handling the
transfer of a tavern's liquor license to a site within 500
feet of Columbia School, despite the protests of the PTA.
It also opposed Army Armstrong, who was setting up a
beer parlor in Bellevue despite local opposition.

O'Brien had no such political albatross around his own neck. But he had a graver problem: he was overconfident. He did not work very hard in the primary campaign. "I had a whole list of people we didn't mail to," he said. "That might have made a difference." Instead of keeping his own fences mended, he was drawn into an attempt to unseat Army Armstrong. Tension had grown between him and Armstrong after he replaced the older man on the powerful Rules Committee. And O'Brien was favored by people who figured Armstrong was too radical.

In addition, there was another strong Irish Catholic House candidate in the primary, a former streetcar motorman named Charles M. Carroll, widely referred to as "Streetcar Charlie." Carroll had recently gained notoriety in a losing race for the Seattle City Council. (He was subsequently a councilman for many years.)

"The left-wing group went out and opposed me," O'Brien said. "They knew Armstrong and I weren't getting along." For the same reason, "a lot of my people supported Carroll. But Carroll supporters didn't support me."

As if that were not enough, the Municipal League said O'Brien had an "unimpressive legislative record." (The League had nothing to say about Carroll. It called Armstrong an "opportunist; left wing.") Closer to home, the editor of a new community newspaper had started referring to him derisively as "Pow Wow John" O'Brien. Some of his campaign signs were torn down. It was not a good omen. When the votes were counted, O'Brien finished third, just twenty-three votes behind "Streetcar Charlie" Carroll. He would not even be on the November ballot. "I defeated myself, more or less," he said.

If he had made it through the primary, he would have gone to Olympia again; even in what turned out to be a

Republican landslide, the 33rd District stayed solidly Democratic. Armstrong, Carroll, and Rosellini were all elected. But the Republicans took both houses of Congress, and they gained firm control of the Washington House. The legislature that met in 1947 was to be very, very conservative. If O'Brien had to lose one election, that may have been the one to lose. There would be little opportunity in the House for a New Deal Democrat to influence policy; little opportunity for an ambitious young Democratic politician to rise.

The Republicans had two-thirds of the House. Through a coalition with eight conservative Democrats, they also controlled the senate. They started the session by overriding Wallgren's vetoes of four bills from 1945, and they soon set about dismantling the state's social welfare system. The 1947 legislature's main claim to fame, though, was its establishment of a committee to investigate un-American activities. While O'Brien was not there to vote on the committee's creation, he would play a key role in blocking future legislative efforts to duplicate it. Ultimately, he would be instrumental in discrediting its chairman and its legacy.

Anticommunism had been a theme in the previous election, and it had not been forgotten after the votes were counted. In December the *Seattle Post-Intelligencer* published a front-page story by Fred Niendorff announcing that a coalition of senate Republicans and Democrats had discussed an investigation. Niendorff himself was credited by some people with drafting the bill that set up a Joint Legislative Fact-Finding Committee on Un-American Activities. Actually, it was patterned on a bill passed by the California legislature in 1945. It was introduced in the House by two freshman legislators, Albert F. Canwell and

Sydney A. Stevens. Canwell, who chaired the committee, had been a deputy sheriff in Spokane County, where he was in charge of the County Identification Bureau. He claimed his experience in the sheriff's office and his conversations with federal agents had led him to favor an investigation.

The legislature might have established anyway what came to be known as the Canwell Committee, but late in the session, radical and liberal groups made it all but inevitable. As the legislature neared adjournment, the capitol was beseiged by around 1,000 members of a "people's march" demanding an increase in the old-age pension to $60 a month, a veterans' bonus, increased aid to public schools, and a fair employment practices act—a list reminiscent of John O'Brien's primary platform in 1946. The Pension Union had already held a demonstration at the capitol to promote the $60 minimum pension. This time, chartered buses from all over western Washington disgorged people carrying banners and placards. Communist banners were visible, but clearly, not all the demonstrators were communists. A dozen veterans, demonstrating for the bonus, pitched pup tents on the capitol lawn. There were speeches on the capitol steps, and the accompanying cheers could be heard by the legislators inside. Twenty-five demonstrators were thrown out of the senate gallery after one had shouted that the senators were giving the veterans' bonus issue "a run-around." Another group tried to get into the House gallery but found the doors closed. The demonstrators banged on the doors and yelled, "Open the door, Richard!" Both houses quickly recessed, passing resolutions that no one should be let in for another two hours. The demonstrators tried to force their way into the senate chamber. But the door held. Just how much of a menace the demonstrators posed was largely in the eye of the beholder. Niendorff described "a screaming, howling mob of men and women who earlier in the day had displayed Communist banners on the capitol steps," trying to "force their way into both legislative galleries."

Two days later, the House approved an investigation of un-American activities by a vote of 86 to 6. "Things occurring during this session make the need for this investigation self-evident," Canwell said. "The leaders of these groups know that the power to tax is the power to destroy. They are trying to lay the foundation for revolution."

Army Armstrong, one of the eight Democrats who opposed the resolution, quoted Abraham Lincoln in reply: "We were born in revolution. God help us if we ever lose the right of revolution."

Armstrong's was not the prevailing sentiment. Charles Carroll said, "It would not be a waste of money if the state spent a million dollars to prevent the communists from driving a wedge into our government."

What O'Brien would have said if he had been there is anyone's guess. He was certainly no friend of the left— he had won the primary endorsement of an anticommunist group—but he was not a Red baiter, and he was not given to ideological hysterics.

The Canwell Committee held two hearings in 1948. The first looked primarily at the Washington Pension Union. The second looked at alleged communist influence at the University of Washington. Canwell's assault on the university was "the first, and in many ways the most important, academic freedom case of the entire cold war," writes Ellen W. Schrecker in *No Ivory Tower: McCarthyism and the*

Universities (Oxford, 1986). Faculty members were asked to inform on their colleagues. Students were asked about their teachers. There were rumors of agents planted in classrooms. Even before the hearings started, the Washington campus was rife with suspicion. The hearings themselves were inquisitional. There was no right to cross-examine witnesses. Professional anticommunists held forth on the suspicious nature of groups joined by people like Albert Einstein.

As a result of the hearings, the university fired three tenured faculty members, two of whom actually were Communist party members, and put three others on probation. Other people were damaged by innuendo, and at least one man, University of Washington philosophy teacher Melvin Rader, was subsequently found to have been framed. Ed Guthman of the *Seattle Times* won a Pulitzer Prize for laying out the facts of the Rader case. As O'Brien said, the Canwell Committee investigations "hurt a lot of people."

The hearings formed part of the political environment in which O'Brien had to fight his way back into the state legislature. The university hearings began around filing time for the September primary. By then, the first strike in Boeing's thirty-two-year history had already dragged on for three months. Lodge 751 of the Boeing aeronautical workers, for which O'Brien still audited the books, had struck, partly over money—workers wanted another thirty cents an hour; Boeing offered only fifteen cents—partly over seniority rights.

The seniority clause in the old contract prevented the company from either assigning employees as it liked or keeping the employees it valued most as the work force

contracted after World War II. Boeing President William
Allen said the company could afford neither the seniority
provisions nor the thirty-cent-an-hour raise. He claimed
that by striking without warning, the union had lost its
rights as a bargaining agent.

The company sued the union. The union accused Boeing
of an unfair labor practice. Dave Beck, leader of the West
Coast Teamsters and pillar of the Seattle and state political establishments (the conservative state senate of 1947
confirmed his appointment to the University of Washington Board of Regents) started a rival union for Boeing
workers. The company hired nonunion labor. The strike
finally caved in that September. Workers voted to go back
to work without a contract. The union surrendered on
seniority.

September brought a different moment of truth—the
primary vote—to John O'Brien. There was no indication
that the conservative tide had turned, and there was every
reason to believe that the legislature—and the U.S. presidency—would go to the Republicans. But the 33rd District had not forsaken the Democrats; there, the primary
remained the main event.

This time, O'Brien went out and worked. He spent a
lot of time campaigning. He called on his ties to the unions.
He spent roughly twice as much money as he had in 1946,
using $25.75 of it to buy 10,000 throwaway leaflets.

The effort paid off. O'Brien got a place on the November ballot alongside Charles Carroll. Army Armstrong
finished a distant third. Armstrong's big political venture
that year was testifying as a former communist before the
Canwell Committee.

When the votes were counted in November, O'Brien
had "led the ticket," getting more votes than any other

33rd District candidate. He wound up with 8,820 votes, 1,033 more than Carroll. The only break in his legislative career was over. For most of the next four decades, his reelection would be routine.

Much to almost everyone's surprise, the 1948 election was not a replay of 1946. There was no Republican sweep. Although the *Chicago Tribune* printed an election-night headline proclaiming Republican candidate Thomas E. Dewey the new president, the winner was Democrat Harry Truman. And in Washington, although Langlie returned to the governor's mansion, the Democrats won a majority in the House.

The stage was set for O'Brien to take another try at the Speakership. And try he did. Right after the election, Lodge 751 voted to endorse him, and Lodge President Harold J. Gibson wrote that "we have always found him to be liberal and a staunch supporter of true Democratic principles. We actively supported him during his recent campaign and we would now like to recommend him for election to the vitally important post of Speaker."

It was already too late. Charles Hodde, who had served in the 1947 legislature, had slipped in ahead of him. Hodde was an eastern Washington farmer who had worked on the Grange initiatives for a public utility district law and a state income tax in 1930 and 1932. He had led the isolated House Democrats during the 1947 session and, during the election of 1948, he had helped a lot of Democratic legislators with their campaigns. Hodde had expected the Republicans to carry the House that year, too. When the returns started coming in on election night, and he saw that they would not, he realized that he had a chance to be Speaker. He did not go to bed that night. Instead, he spent the night on the telephone, calling victorious

Democrats all over the state—most of them, transfixed by the returns, had not gone to bed, either—and asking for their support. By the next day, Hodde had lined up enough votes to become Speaker. O'Brien would have to wait for a different year.

Illustrations

At the rostrum: Speaker of the House John L. O'Brien *(Greg Gilbert photo)*.

Top left: Mr. and Mrs. James O'Brien, ca. 1910. James Thomas O'Brien and Mary Margaret Manning came to the United States from Cork and Kilkenny, respectively. *Top right:* City Detective James O'Brien, 1919. *Lower left:* John O'Brien, 1955 *(Walters Studio). Lower right:* John L. and Mary Schwartz O'Brien, 1952.

From the Seattle *Post-Intelligencer*, 23 January 1921: "Victims of Bandit's Bullets.
1. Three of Detective O'Brien's children, grouped behind the baby's crib, in which is
Mary Josephine, 2 months old. Left to right – James Thomas, Wilford Martin, and
John Lawrence. *(Webster & Stevens)* 2. City Detective James O'Brien. 3. Mrs. James
O'Brien. 4. The new bungalow, which the O'Brien family has lived in but three
months and which Mr. O'Brien helped build while off duty. *(Webster & Stevens, Times
Staff Photographers)*"

The O'Brien family, 1988. *Left to right,* John, Sr., Mary, Laurie, John, Jr., Mary Ann, Karen, Jeannie, Paul *(courtesy* Seattle Times, *Greg Gilbert photo).*

Campaign 1988 – solid support from grandson Michael and John, Jr. *(courtesy* Seattle Times, *Greg Gilbert photo).*

Top: "The fastest gavel north of the Pecos!" *(Weekly Olympian)* *Bottom:* Sharing the rostrum – a proud grandfather with Sean and Michael, 1988. *(courtesy* Seattle Times)

Top: Unveiling the Mother Joseph statue in the Capitol, Washington, D.C., 1979. Sister Lucille Dean, provincial superior, Sacred Heart Province, and Sister Michelle Holland, provincial superior, St. Ignatius Province. *Bottom:* With Pope Pius XII, 1958, The Vatican. *Left to right,* Ethyl Rosellini, Governor Albert Rosellini, John O'Brien, Mary O'Brien, Sarah Weisfeld, Leo Weisfeld.

Left: Honoring Rabbi Raphael Levine, Olympia, 1981. *Left to right,* O'Brien, Rabbi Levine, House Page Paul O'Brien, Father William Treacy.

Right: With Representative P. J. (Jim) Gallagher, honoring Archbishop Raymond G. Hunthausen, Olympia, 1987 *(Ed Kane photo).*

After the signing of the Kosher food bill, 1985. *Left to right,* O'Brien, Rabbi Moses Londinski, Rabbi William Greenberg, Rabbi Simon Benzaquen, Governor Booth Gardner, and Rabbi Mordechai Londinski *(Ed Kane photo).*

Left: A good neighbor – working with the South Seattle Crime Prevention Council, 1988.

Above: O'Brien was one of the original sponsors of the act providing legislative support for building the convention center.

Above: With Sarah A. Lynch, age ninety-plus, at the Central Area Senior Citizens building, 1988.

Right: Discussing the construction of adequate I-90 access, 1988, with Joe Benton, president of the Urban Business Association, and Steve Shulman, president of the Leschi Community Council.

Left: With Governor Dan Evans and Francis J. Walker, general counsel, Washington Catholic Conference, 1968.

Right: With Governor Dixy Lee Ray and, *left to right,* Representatives Shirley Winsley, Dr. A. A. Adams, and Gene Lux, 1979.

Below: With Governor Booth Gardner and House Majority Leader Brian Ebersole, 1987 *(Ed Kane photo).*

Above: Presentation of the bust of George Washington, commissioned by the Mother Joseph Foundation, 1984. Lieut. Governor John A. Cherberg, O'Brien, Charlotte Naccarato, sculptor Avard Fairbanks, and Governor John Spellman.

Left: With United States Senator Henry M. (Scoop) Jackson, 1968 *(Louis Staudt photo)*.

Right: With United States Senator Warren G. Magnuson, 1968 *(Louis Staudt photo)*.

A gathering of the clan: Former Speakers of the House assemble for a rare historic portrait, 1986. *Standing, left to right,* Leonard Sawyer, Don Eldridge, John Bagnariol, Robert Schaefer, Wayne Ellers, Thomas Swayze; *seated, left to right,* Charles Hodde, John O'Brien, John Sylvester.

Left: With Congresswoman Julia Butler Hansen and State Representative Newman Clark, 1963. *(Ron Allen photo)*

Below: Receiving the Hawaiian Bowl from House Speaker Tadao Beppu of the Hawaii State Legislature, Honolulu, 1968. *(Island Camera)*

t the fiftieth Rainier District Pow Wow, 1983. *Left to right,* John Merrill, Sybil ishimee, Princess Corinda Lee Woods, Princess Denise Andres, Queen Anita Jo anada, David Merrill, Seattle Mayor Charles Royer, John O'Brien.

Left: With Paul Leistner, the first recipient of the John L. O'Brien Post-Graduate Legislative Fellowship, and Representative Ken Jacobsen, chairman, House Higher Education Committee, 1989 *(Ed Kane photo)*.

Right: With 1988 recipients of the Washington State Medal of Merit Award. *Left to right,* Helen Hardin Jackson for her late husband, Sen. Henry M. Jackson; Dr. William Hutchinson; and Edward E. Carlson.

John O'Brien holding the first of his classes in parliamentary procedure for freshman legislators, Olympia, 1971. *Left to right,* Peggy Joan Maxie, Jim McDermott, David Ceccarelli, H. Stan Bradley, Dan Van Dyke, Al Bauer, Jeff Douthwaite, King Lysen. Not visible are Donn Charnley and Ed Luders.

THE WHITE HOUSE

March 15, 1989

ear Mr. Speaker:

am pleased to extend my warm congratulations on the
0th anniversary of your first election to the Washington
ouse of Representatives, especially as your beloved
vergreen State celebrates its Centennial.

his is a proud and historic moment for you, your con-
tituents and colleagues, because rarely in the history
f our country has a person served his fellow citizens
ith such distinction for so many years. During a tenure
panning ten Presidencies -- from Franklin Roosevelt's
 my own -- you have witnessed and been a participant
 some of the great events of our century. Your legis-
tive skill and able handling of each of the major House
adership posts have won you the lasting esteem of
ur colleagues on both sides of the aisle. And your
nstituents? They just keep electing you.

r. Speaker, you're an inspiration to all who serve this
eat country. Barbara and the entire Bush family join
e in sending best wishes.

Sincerely,

Ge Bush

e Honorable John L. O'Brien
eaker pro tempore of the House
 of Representatives of
 the State of Washington
ympia, Washington

Left: An Irish toast "Slainta!" Wielding the shillelagh presented to him by House Speaker Ralph Munro on John O'Brien Recognition Day March 17, 1989.

State of Washington

John L. O'Brien Building

1989

Washington State House of Representatives Resolution 89-4638 Building Name Change

State Capitol Committee

Honorable Booth Gardner, Governor
Honorable Joel Pritchard, Lt. Governor
Honorable Brian Boyle, Commissioner of Public Lands

Department of General Administration
K. Wendy Holden

Above: Mr. and Mrs. O'Brien being congratulated by Representative Gary Locke and State Senator George Fleming on Recognition Day. Mrs. O'Brien was named Honorary First Lady of the Washington House of Representatives.

Governor Booth Gardner proclaimed March 17, 1989, John L. O'Brien Recognition Day, honoring O'Brien's nearly fifty years of public service. A highlight was the renaming of the House Office Building in Olympia as the John L. O'Brien Building *(Ed Kane photo)*.

The State of Washington

Proclamation

WHEREAS, John L. O'Brien is serving his 25th term in the Washington State House of Representatives, the longest tenure of anyone in Washington state history; and

WHEREAS, during his distinguished legislative career, Representative O'Brien served four consecutive terms as Speaker of the House of Representatives, also a record; and

WHEREAS, Representative O'Brien has served on all of the major legislative committees, many interim committees and other distinguished legislative bodies; and

WHEREAS, Representative O'Brien knows more about the members of the Legislature and the creation of state law than most of us will ever learn and, therefore, has some great stories to tell; and

WHEREAS, some of his past and present colleagues probably wish he would, in fact, forget certain details of the past; and

WHEREAS, his compatriots in the House of Representatives have chosen St. Patrick's Day to honor a most responsible consumer of the beverage that we closely identify with his ancestral homeland of Ireland; and

WHEREAS, in all seriousness, John L. O'Brien will be remembered by all future Washingtonians as the namesake for the House Office Building in Olympia, which will be known from this day forward as the John L. O'Brien House Office Building;

NOW, THEREFORE, I, Booth Gardner, Governor of the State of Washington, do hereby proclaim March 17, 1989, as

John L. O'Brien
Recognition Day

in the State of Washington, and I urge all citizens to give a tip o' the cap to Representative John L. O'Brien. Johnny, we're glad to know you.

Signed, this 17th day of March, 1989

Governor Booth Gardner

JOSEPH E. KING
SPEAKER
OF THE HOUSE

June 28, 1989

Speaker Pro Tempore John L. O'Brien
1305 Joseph Vance Building
Seattle, Washington 98101

Dear John,

With the perspective that comes from a little time and distanc
from the Legislature, I feel more than ever that our caucus ha
an incredibly successful session. We truly were the caucus tha
was willing to take the risks, build a progressive agenda ar
change the world -- at least our corner of the world -- and
think that's what our constituents hired us to do!

Apparently forever, Mr. Speaker, you remain a key part of ou
leadership efforts to help develop an agenda. Your advice ar
guidance is always appreciated. I am always mindful of t
incredible perspective you bring to bear on this progress.

Thank you for your continued support.

Best,

JOSEPH E. KING
Speaker

JEK:kln

III

The Gavel at Last

WITH MANY YEARS' HINDSIGHT, CHARLES HODDE SAYS the 1949 session was the first modern legislature in Washington State's history. It was the first to deal primarily with the state as it emerged from the great changes of World War II, moving past the issues of the Great Depression. (It was also the first to vote its successors an appreciable salary. Future legislators would get $100-a-month year round. O'Brien was a member of the Conference Committee that approved the salary.)

But the legislature of 1949 did not start with a clean slate. It had inherited heavy financial obligations. The marchers who had helped stampede the 1947 legislature into setting up the Canwell Committee had been demanding a veterans' bonus and a higher old-age pension. The conservative legislature had wanted no part of those demands. But the state had had a $120-million surplus, and the people had put enough names on initiative petitions to place both the pension increase and the veterans' bonus on the ballot in November 1948. Both initiatives had passed. The voters who had elected the first modern legislature also had passed the last of the big social spending initiatives that grew from the ideas and sensibilities of the Depression.

Given a golden opportunity to let one of the initiatives die, the new legislators hurriedly revived it. The state supreme court had quickly declared the veterans' bonus initiative unconstitutional; the bonus was to be financed with thirty-year bonds, but the state constitution forbade bonds with terms longer than twenty years. The previous legislature might have welcomed its judicial good fortune; the 1949 legislature promptly passed a new bonus bill that relied on twenty-year bonds. The veterans' bonus had become a motherhood issue. But that did not make the state's pockets any deeper. By the time the legislators reached Olympia in 1949, the pension initiative had already devoured the surplus. How to pay off the twenty-year bonds was the big question. The answer was, by taxing sin a little more heavily: the state would get the money by doubling the cigarette tax.

O'Brien, as vice-chairman of the Appropriations Committee, was in the thick of the efforts to pay for everything. "I practically ran that committee," he recalled. "the chairman, Ed Riley [not the former Speaker], was far more conservative than the Democratic caucus, so I handled all the policy matters for the Democratic caucus. I more or less fronted for the Democratic side" on appropriations.

Being on the Appropriations Committee put O'Brien in the center of the House power structure. Appropriations and Highways were the two great dispensers of pork. O'Brien's friend and seatmate, Julia Butler Hansen, had just become the nation's first woman chairman of a Highways Committee. Although money was tight, 1949 was a big year for highway spending. The state's highways needed repairs; they had been deteriorating all through the 1940s.

There were also new projects to tempt the legislature; the final highway appropriation included $4 million to build the Alaskan Way Viaduct through downtown Seattle. The full appropriation totalled $107,616,633. In the days before a Washington State Highway Commission, that was all money to be given out at least partly on the basis of partisan considerations. Hansen understood the system well. After the highway bill had been put together, she discovered that it included nothing that had been asked for by the Speaker. She went to Hodde and said, "Charlie, there's nothing in there for you." Hodde put in a bridge over the Pend Oreille River, in his own district. It became known as "the Speaker's bridge."

Everyone could find a use for the money the state no longer had. The schools needed money, too. Clayton Farrington of the Washington State Federation of Teachers wrote the next year that, in addition to voting for the veterans' bonus and the teachers' tenure law, and against both a flat-rate income tax and an increase in the sales tax, O'Brien had fought hard for an amendment that would have added another $17 million to the appropriation for public schools. "He [O'Brien] joined with me and his seatmate, Julia Butler Hansen, in supporting this, talking for it and voting for it." O'Brien also fought for it in conference, but to no avail.

O'Brien himself remembered sitting on a conference committee in 1949, trying to get extra money in the budget for schools. The conferees "met in the Senate Appropriations Committee room at night for a whole week, and Pearl Wanamaker, who was superintendent of public instruction, would wait for me out in the rotunda, and Charlie Hodde [would wait] in the Speaker's office. The two of them used to wait until we finished at night to find out how I was doing in the conference committee. It would be around eleven o'clock when we would adjourn."

New ways of raising money were few and far between. The legislature authorized spending $470 million against revenues of $396 million.

Some legislators worried less about money matters than they did about communism. The Canwell Committee was gone but not forgotten; the sentiments that had inspired it were still very much alive in some quarters. For instance, when the legislative session began, Charles W. Doyle, secretary of the Seattle Central Labor Council, urged the legislators to keep on investigating subversive activities. Doyle also told the American Federation of Labor board: "American trade unionists are watching with keenest interest the activities of the various members of the legislature as to what position they will take when this important matter comes up for decision."

The following month, when former Governor Mon Wallgren was nominated to be chairman of the federal National Security Resources Board, Senator Harry P. Cain, who had been elected in the conservative landslide of 1946, proclaimed: "During the term of office of Mon Wallgren the entire state administration came under the control of persons whose first allegiance was to the Kremlin."

Most legislators thought the Canwell Committee's revival, in one form or another, was a foregone conclusion. The House authorized a watered-down version of it. The senate passed a stronger version. In conference, the House refused to go along with the senate. A conference committee got nowhere. A new investigation of un-American activities still seemed inevitable, but with the House and senate unable to agree, it could not happen for another two years.

Although the 1949 legislature could not agree on investigating communism at home, it did manage to take rhetorical stands on fighting communism abroad. It passed O'Brien's resolutions commending President Truman for sending military aid to South Korea and for condemning the Hungarian government's persecution of the country's highest-ranking Catholic clergyman, Joseph Cardinal Mindszenty.

O'Brien told his still largely Catholic constituents about the Mindszenty resolution in a letter during the 1950 election campaign. By that time, the South Korea resolution was somewhat beside the point; North Korean troops had crossed the 38th parallel, and the United States was embroiled in a full-fledged Korean War.

O'Brien was reelected handily in 1950. The whole campaign cost him less than $1,000. His American Oil Company contributed $200 to the campaign; the state's CPAs, $150; the Washington Restaurant Association, $50. O'Brien's old seatmate, Army Armstrong, tried to make a comeback in the primary. Armstrong's time had passed, though, and his testimony before the Canwell Committee could not have endeared him to the people who had once been his strongest supporters. Armstrong did not make it. The 33rd District delegation still consisted of O'Brien, Albert Rosellini, and Charles Carroll.

The 1950 election broke the chain of social spending initiatives. The voters rejected the Pension Union's Initiative 176, which would have liberalized the state's welfare system—opponents argued that coming on the heels of the Pension Union's previous initiative, it would bankrupt the state—and passed Langlie's Initiative 178, which tightened up eligibility for welfare. (Langlie made much of fiscal responsibility throughout his career.) Voters in

Seattle's 37th District also elected the state legislature's first black member, Charles M. Stokes. (A black representative had served in the territorial legislature, but none had served since statehood.)

When the legislators reached Olympia, they found a state capitol still showing the effects of a powerful earthquake that had shaken it right after the legislature had adjourned in 1949. In April 1949, the chief clerk of the House, Si Holcomb, wrote to O'Brien, "It is a marvel to all of us that the Capitol still stands, considering the way it rocked, twisted and moved around during the interminable period of the earthquake. We have all been ordered out of the building . . . and are now located in the basement of the Governor Hotel."

The capitol still stood. So did O'Brien's determination to be Speaker. But he had Charles Hodde to contend with. Hodde wrote to O'Brien right after the November election, "I would like to have you in the 'front row' this time. I would like to serve as Speaker again."

That was how it turned out. Hodde still had enough votes in the Democratic caucus to beat O'Brien, 30 to 17. But O'Brien had by that time developed into a powerful rival who could not simply be shunted aside—not under the circumstances of 1951. The Democrats had only a nine-vote majority. Some Democrats felt Hodde had been too autocratic a Speaker in 1949. If four or more of them followed a disgruntled leader to the Republican side, Hodde would be left high and dry. Normally, a politician who challenged the Speaker and lost would have been ostracized. Instead, O'Brien was elected chairman of the Democratic caucus and served as majority floor leader.

The idea of dissident Democrats making common cause with Republicans was not at all farfetched: the senate was

already being run by a coalition of Republicans and conservative Democrats, as it had been in 1949. Washington
Water Power, the private utility that served the Spokane
area, had been instrumental in setting up the coalition.

The public utility districts' right to condemn private
utility property was, understandably, a major issue for the
private utilities. At one point in the early 1950s, *all* Puget
Power's holdings faced condemnation. Initiatives that would
have restricted the PUDs' right to condemn were voted
down in 1940 and 1946. After that, private power tried
to alter state law by influencing the legislature rather than
the people.

In the 1951 session, private power pinned a lot of hopes
on the amended version of the so-called Spokane Power
Bill. The eastern holding company that owned Washington Water Power was being forced by federal law to sell
it. Former Senator Clarence Dill, attorney for the Pend
Oreille PUD in eastern Washington, thought this provided a perfect opportunity for "the extinction of the
Washington Water Power Company." Under his plan,
several PUDs would buy a majority of the company's stock.
The PUDs would take over Washington Water Power operations in the rural areas. The City of Spokane would
take over the urban part of the system. The power bill,
as originally written, enabled Spokane to take over Washington Water Power operations within the city.

The triumph of public power in the Spokane area
seemed imminent. During debate in the House, Representative C. A. Orndorff of Spokane offered a resolution
proposing that Spokane County secede from the state of
Washington and join Idaho, because Washington was "becoming too socialistic."

The amendment to the power bill, tacked on by the

senate, was designed to stop the public power takeover. It required a vote of the people in Spokane before the city could acquire the electrical system.

When the senate amendment reached the House, O'Brien moved not to concur. The debate was already heated when Representative Kenneth H. Simmons interrupted on a point of personal privilege. Simmons dropped a bombshell, claiming that he and Representative Reuben A. Knoblauch had been offered $25 apiece by a man named John Uleman to vote for the bill. Simmons said the bribery attempt had been recorded verbatim by a stenographer hidden behind a bookcase in a committee meeting room. Simmons said, "Not ten minutes ago, Knoblauch and I walked into the men's lounge and approached [Uleman] who [had] asked us to come off the floor. I said, 'What's the deal?'"

Uleman allegedly replied, "There will be $25 in cash for both of you if you vote yes on House Bill 557 as it came from the senate."

"I asked him where the money came from, and he replied: 'This is not my money; it is Spokane power money.'"

The House was thrown into an uproar. Hodde came down from the rostrum to speak, his voice breaking with emotion. "This is probably the most serious matter that has been brought before this legislature since I have served here," Hodde said. "I want to tell this House that big men, honest men, have come into my office and cried—cried like children—because they couldn't stand up under the pressure that has been put upon them."

Afterward, O'Brien felt that the incident itself had been relatively trivial. What had made it stand out was Hodde's emotional response. O'Brien felt, with hindsight, that Hodde had been wrong to come down from the rostrum to make an impassioned statement on the floor. In his view, Hodde's emotional involvement had detracted from the dignity of the Speakership.

The bribery incident disrupted the flow of House business only briefly, but it may well have helped to doom the senate amendment to the Spokane Power Bill. After the House adjourned that day, a Spokane representative, W. Kennott Jones, said that "the amendments put on in the senate would have been approved in the House if seven Democrats had not run for cover after the bribery charge was made."

The power fight turned out to be moot. Washington Water Power had operations across the state line—in Idaho—and so Washington public utilities could not legally acquire it. The PUDs had planned to sell the Idaho operations immediately, beating the law through fast footwork. The ploy did not work; the bond broker who arranged the financing told the mayor of Spokane, who tipped off the attorney for Washington Water Power, who got an injunction in time to wreck the scheme.

Another legislative failure was a landmark urban renewal bill, introduced by O'Brien and Charles M. Stokes. The proposed bill would have let cities use eminent domain to clear and redevelop blighted areas. But in 1951, urban renewal was just getting started in the United States, and Washington was not ready to accept it.

O'Brien's bill to set up a new 7th Congressional District fared only marginally better. The census of 1950 had entitled Washington to another congressman. At issue was how to draw the boundary line. The Democrats wanted to lump largely Democratic Kitsap County in with a King County district. Republicans wanted to include it in the 2nd Congressional District, where they figured Democrat

Henry Jackson was unbeatable anyway. The bill that O'Brien introduced was described as shameless Democratic gerrymandering, but it passed. The Republican governor vetoed it.

Money was still a big concern, with no end of things to spend it on and no easy way of getting more. Dr. Edward L. Turner, dean of the University of Washington Medical School, warned that the school "might as well be discontinued" unless the legislature provided money to build a teaching hospital. The superintendent of public instruction wanted $45 million more for the public schools. O'Brien introduced a bill that would provide another $3 million for teachers' pay. The smallest welfare budget anyone envisioned was still $12 million above Governor Langlie's projections.

Initiative 178, passed in 1950, had saved the state money on welfare payments, but some of its savings had been illusory, and others might soon go by the boards. The legislature set up a committee to investigate the postinitiative practices of the Welfare Department. O'Brien explained, "We are dissatisfied with the department's practices under Initiative 178, and we want to correct abuses before they go too far." He said welfare recipients reportedly had had their checks reduced by up to $25 a month because they owned cars.

Primarily to pay for increased welfare costs, Governor Langlie was pushing a 4-percent corporate income tax. It was to be a familiar pattern: no useful distinction was made between tax reform and tax increase, so the public was appropriately hostile; the Republicans believed a person who succeeded financially should not pay a larger percentage of his income to the government than anyone else, so they favored a flat-rate tax; some Democrats clung to the egalitarian principle that those who had the most should pay the most, and they held out for a graduated income tax. For some Democrats, *no* income tax was preferable to a flat-rate tax—or to any tax dreamed up by Republicans. From the start, O'Brien believed that a graduated tax was the fairest way for the state to collect funds. During the 1951 session, he became a spokesman for a group of Democrats who opposed Langlie and favored a graduated income tax. The Democratic House defeated the 4-percent corporate income tax two days in a row.

The trouble was that the Democrats had no chance of passing a graduated tax, and no one had a better idea for raising money. The legislature sold bonds to begin building the University of Washington Hospital and for more than $66 million worth of highway improvements, but those were capital costs, not operating expenses. In April, nearly four months into what was to have been a sixty-day session, the legislature was still wrestling with the task of getting enough money to run the state. O'Brien was one of three House and three senate members appointed to a conference committee to work out a solution. Their decision was to go for a 4-percent corporate tax, after all, and to combine the budget and the revenue measure in a single bill. It was the first and only income tax the legislature passed after the Depression. The state supreme court quickly found—to no one's great surprise—that addressing two different purposes in a single bill was unconstitutional. The court termed the legislature's final solution a "two-headed monster." The corporate income tax died with the rest of the legislation. It was not revived. Instead, the legislature increased a variety of minor taxes—enough to make up some, but not all, of the expected deficit.

The financial crisis was not the only concern inherited from the previous legislature. The desire to investigate un-American activities remained in some legislative hearts. Although the previous session had not passed a bill renewing the Canwell Committee investigations, legislators felt that the passage of a similar bill might be inevitable. Langlie, who had long been concerned about communist influence, could not be expected to veto a new investigation. The opposition strategy was not to kill an investigation, which might prove impossible, but to add some safeguards and to water it down. After a bill was introduced in the House, O'Brien proposed amendments that would let the Speaker of the House appoint the committee's chairman (Hodde was not a fan of the investigation), would permit public hearings only at the request of the attorney general (the attorney general was a Democrat), and would permit only the attorney general to conduct investigations. The amendments, said O'Brien, would "stop any member of the committee from going off on a tangent or . . . conducting a witch hunt."

The senate rejected the House amendments.

The senators passed a bill with amendments of their own, which the House rejected 53 to 46. Conservative Republican Perry Woodall pointed out that the senate had passed the bill 44 to 0; he suggested that the House "would do well to give its approval."

O'Brien disagreed. "I'm not pleased with what the senate has done this session," he said. "They're supposed to be economy-minded over there, but the first thing I notice about their amendment is that they've raised the appropriation from $100,000 to $150,000." O'Brien the accountant could sidestep the ideological issues and attack the conservatives for not being conservative enough. But the pragmatic approach worked. The House refused to accept the Senate version, and the legislation died, never to be seriously reconsidered.

The next year, Charles Hodde made the mistake of thinking that his prominence within the legislature could easily be translated into prominence outside it. He gave up his seat to pursue the Democratic nomination for governor. He lost. No Speaker has yet gone on to win a higher office. Dan Evans, who became governor and then U.S. senator, was a Republican leader in the House, but he was never Speaker.

Hodde's departure cleared the way for O'Brien. Or it might have if the election of 1952, in which Dwight D. Eisenhower was elected president by an overwhelming majority over Adlai Stevenson, had not been a Republican sweep. O'Brien himself won reelection easily. Assessing candidates before the election, the Municipal League said O'Brien was "inclined to follow a middle course on measures involving higher taxes or expenditures."

The election of 1952 left the Republicans in control of both houses of the legislature, as well as the governor's mansion, where Langlie would spend another four years. The new Speaker was O'Brien's friend, Seattle printing company owner Mort Frayn. O'Brien himself was defeated for the post of caucus chairman by another friend, Julia Butler Hansen, but he was elected minority floor leader.

For the first time in O'Brien's legislative career, his party was in the minority. He found it frustrating. "I like being in the majority," he once said. "Being in the minority isn't all that pleasant."

At the start of the session, a newspaper described O'Brien as "brisk and watchful. . . . [He] generally wears a completely sober expression, but when he smiles it is like a little burst of Irish sunshine."

He must have smiled a lot at the Republican majority's failure to get its own bills passed. O'Brien's role as a Democratic floor leader was largely to obstruct. "I suppose at that time I was a very militant floor leader," he said later. "We went out to attack and defeat bills prepared by the opposition. . . . They used to say that when they'd see me with the red book [*Reed's Rules of Order*] out, they knew that some problem was going to be developing."

Although O'Brien considered Frayn a fair speaker, Frayn could not control some members of his own caucus, so he could not get the Republicans to vote as a reliable block. The Democrats, who were better organized, managed to keep them from passing bills. "Frayn had a package of bills on reorganization," O'Brien recalled (the blue-ribbon Shefelman Commission had come out with recommendations for reorganizing state government) "and we killed them all. We were in the minority. Mort Frayn told me that one time the governor called and said, 'You're the worst Speaker the state ever had.' And Mort just laughed at him."

Reorganization was not the only Republican plan that went down to defeat. The Republicans tried, as the Constitution required, to redistrict the state in light of the 1950 census. Redistricting had always evoked such intense conflicts of partisanship and self-interest that no twentieth-century legislature had ever accomplished it, except when forced to in 1930 by an initiative that increased the number of legislative seats. The legislature of 1953 was no exception, although if O'Brien had been less obstinately partisan, it might have been. The Republicans put together redistricting bills, but the House and senate passed different versions. Their fate was left up to a free conference committee, one member of which was John O'Brien. O'Brien simply stalled the bills to death. "We weren't going to approve that redistricting bill at all," he recalled. "I remember Vic Zednick was chairman of the committee, and he couldn't get me to agree. I would keep offering different suggestions, recommendations to improve the redistricting measure." Any decision of the committee had to be unanimous. "Six people had to approve," O'Brien said. "I just rode out the clock and it died, even though they controlled both houses."

O'Brien and company also managed to derail another private power bill. Power was still a hot topic in the state. Development of cheap, abundant power in Washington had largely been the work of the federal government, which had built the Columbia River dams. The public utilities depended heavily—many of them exclusively—on that federal power. It was clear that the Eisenhower administration was hostile to the idea of the federal government producing and marketing electricity. Facing a possible end to federal assistance, the legislature made it legal for public utilities jointly to develop their own generating facilities. This was not done in a nonpartisan spirit. Once again, the Democrats were backing public power, and most Republicans were fighting it.

"The record of the [1953] Republican-controlled Legislature is indefensible insofar as public power and power development are concerned," proclaimed a Democratic Elections Committee bulletin prepared by Si Holcomb before the 1954 election. The legislature "has plunged the Northwest and the State of Washington into a complete breakdown of the development of . . . water power."

Holcomb complained that the Republican governor and legislative leaders had told the PUDs and municipal utilities that if they wanted their law, they would have to accept a state power commission, which could be appointed and controlled by the Republicans. He condemned the bargain as "a 'black jack' trade" that public power people accepted because they had no choice.

The biggest fight broke out over another bill that attempted to restrict the freedom of PUDs to condemn private utility property. The bill went through the Public Utilities Committee, where a substitute bill was entered. The Democratic Elections Committee called it "a vicious example of legislative trickery, where two anti-PUD bills were reported out of a Republican private-power-controlled committee without even giving local public power people a chance to appear."

The bills would have to be stopped on the floor. Public power forces thought they would have a better chance of killing the original than the substitute. When the substitute bill came out to be passed and sent to the Rules Committee, O'Brien moved to re-refer it back to Public Utilities. He lost. When the bill came back to the floor from Rules, though, he raised a point of order and won; he got the substitute bill thrown out. Then, he moved to re-refer the original bill. He won by one vote. After the vote, former Speaker Ed Reilly, who was back in the legislature—and who, as a representative from Spokane, was closely tied to private power—moved to reconsider the question. O'Brien clearly enjoyed telling Reilly that when *he* was Speaker, he had ruled that you *couldn't* reconsider a motion to re-refer. Public power had carried the day. O'Brien had learned how to manipulate the parliamentary system.

After the session, it was obvious that O'Brien and Julia Butler Hansen would be the main contenders for Speaker if the Democrats won in 1954. O'Brien had become both a party spokesman and a target for people who were trying to attack the party. The senate Republican co–floor leader, Neil J. Hoff, charged that "it was O'Brien and his party that sponsored welfare Initiative 172 [the 1948 pension increase], which seriously damaged the economy of this state."

The Democrats won the House in the 1954 election, albeit only by a single seat. It was time for O'Brien to make another move for the Speakership. He started well in advance. He phoned legislators, He drove around the state to talk with them. The day before the Democratic caucus met to choose a Speaker, the press reported that O'Brien had been buttonholing legislators left and right.

The caucus fight between O'Brien and Hansen was expected to be close. One O'Brien supporter, Wally Carmichael of Everett, had been hospitalized with a blood clot in his leg. He was driven to Olympia in an ambulance by Snohomish County Coroner Ken Baker and was carried on a stretcher to the meeting, where he lay for hours in his hospital gown. Despite the heroics, Carmichael's vote was not crucial. O'Brien's groundwork had paid off. Nominated by August Mardesich, he defeated Hansen 29 to 21. It looked as if he would be Speaker at long last.

Hansen's supporters had wanted to put an end to the Speaker's dictatorial power to decide who sat on which committees. They had lost the battle but would win the war. Under O'Brien, a Committee on Committees would be established, giving the whole caucus a voice in deciding committee assignments, if not chairmanships. The Speaker remained powerful, but committee assignments were no longer to be governed exclusively by a one-man spoils system. O'Brien's rise to the Speakership coincided with the first formal limit on the Speaker's arbitrary powers.

Meanwhile, his House victory was by no means a sure thing. The Democrats had only a one-vote majority in the House. One defection, one Democratic legislator absent at the wrong time, and the Speaker would be a Republican. O'Brien could not afford to have anything go wrong.

The crucial vote would come on Monday. On Saturday, Representative Margaret Hurley, wife of former legislator Joseph Hurley and part of the slim Democratic majority, was driving from her home in Spokane to Olympia with her husband, four children, and a friend. Near Cle Elum, their car was wrecked. Hurley wound up in the hospital. Her ankle was injured; she could not walk, and the press reported it was "very doubtful" she could make it to Olympia. Without her, the Democrats no longer had a majority. It looked as if Mort Frayn might be Speaker once again.

The vote was so close that O'Brien and Frayn dispensed with the usual chivalry of such occasions. Normally, each man would have voted for the other. This time, each voted for himself. O'Brien still could have hoped for no better than a draw, except that Hurley dramatically came through. She was brought to the House chambers in a wheelchair, a blanket covering her injured legs. Hers was the one vote the Democrats needed. O'Brien was elected Speaker, 50 to 49. That evening the front page of the *Seattle Times* carried a picture of Hurley sitting in her wheelchair and another of O'Brien accepting the gavel from the former chief clerk. O'Brien was smiling broadly. No wonder. Close vote or not, he had just realized his great ambition.

IV

Laying Ghosts of the 1940s

O'BRIEN WAS TO SERVE AS SPEAKER LONGER THAN anyone else in Washington history. He exercised real power, not only controlling debate but also picking committee chairmen. He kept that power not by being the man on the white horse, leading his colleagues off to battle—he was seldom identified with major issues—but by understanding and controlling the machinery. Maybe it was his training as an accountant; whatever it was, he mastered the details. He knew the rules—he made many of them himself—and he knew how to use parliamentary procedure for partisan ends. As chairman of the Rules Committee, he kept track of all pending bills. He knew all the House members, their districts, and what they thought they needed.

Herb Legg, who became Democratic state chairman in the early 1960s, first encountered O'Brien in the early 1950s. Legg remembered O'Brien in those days as "a bit austere." He also recalled that O'Brien knew exactly what was going on, even when he seemed not to notice. Legg, then a lobbyist for automobile dealers, wanted to get a bill out of the Rules Committee. He went to O'Brien for help. "I went in and talked to him," Legg said, "and he just kind of grunted, but in the next day or two, the bill came out."

O'Brien did not manipulate people psychologically; he found middle ground and made deals. A legislator who knew him years later referred to his "honest broker" approach. O'Brien himself recalled that "Julia Butler Hansen once told me I was a natural-born compromiser."

He was proud of his good relationships with Republicans as well as Democrats. He got the leaders of both parties together every morning—something he had picked up in his first session from Ed Reilly—so that everyone knew what was going on. He had his floor leaders go up and down the aisles to see what motions members planned to introduce. He did not want surprises.

Nevertheless, O'Brien was not known or remembered as a conciliatory or impartial Speaker. He was a partisan presiding officer with a sharp tongue and a quick gavel. A later Speaker found that "the people who served with him in his heyday tell stories that make him out to be absolutely despotic, an absolute tyrant." A Republican who worked with O'Brien as a legislator years later, and who came to appreciate his courtesy as well as his knowledge of the rules, once drove to Olympia during O'Brien's Speakership just to see how the legislature worked. He "left that session thinking that was the most hardheaded, unfair individual they could ever have on the rostrum."

"I don't think that's quite true," O'Brien said later. "I had excellent relationships with both sides of the aisle. I certainly would protect our side, but I didn't ride roughshod over the minority party."

"He managed to have a grudging respect for the Republicans," said Bob Greive, the Democratic state senate leader at the time. And "he had a grudging respect for the left-wing Democrats, the big liberals who thought he was too conservative."

A 1955 directory of legislators characterized O'Brien as "adept in legislative procedure, a quiet, gentlemanly type, at times with an air of being proud, but always fair, considerate and unhurried." In his own copy, O'Brien penciled out "an air of being proud."

If his training as an accountant may have given him an eye for details, so his Catholicism may have given him a respect for hierarchy. Certainly he valued the form, as well as the substance, of being Speaker. From the beginning, he had a regard for the dignity and prestige of the House. Nearly two months into the 1955 session, he circulated a memorandum: "For the purpose of preserving order and decorum, the attention of the members of the House is directed to the following rules of the House." He then explained the House rule on decorum, which read in part: "A member called to order shall immediately sit, unless allowed to explain. If [there is] no appeal, the decision of the chair is final. If appealed, the House will decide *without* debate."

O'Brien also showed what would be a continuing interest in the physical arrangement of the House. When he became Speaker, he automatically got his own office, but he was the only member of the House who did. As when he entered the House, committee chairmen could use their committee hearing rooms as *de facto* offices, but other members had only their desks. Most members would not have private offices for nearly two more decades, but O'Brien got $165,000 appropriated to have unused space on the ground floor of the House made into offices for his floor leaders.

O'Brien never denied that he was a strong Speaker. Years

later, someone suggested that procedures had changed so
much that no one could really run the House as it had
once been run. Clearly, O'Brien replied, the current
Speaker could not do it. But it could still be done. "*I* could
run the House," he said.

In 1955, he ran the House with a one-vote margin and
a strong hand. That year's legislature in effect brought
Washington into the mid-twentieth century. It did away
with the spaces for declaring race and religion that had
until then appeared on all state forms. It passed a bill that
would have established a toll road through Seattle from
Everett to Tacoma. (The next year, Congress passed the
federal Interstate Highway Act, making a toll road un-
necessary.) It passed a teacher tenure law. It passed the
first water pollution bill in ten years, requiring companies
discharging wastes into the water to get permits from the
state.

Money was, as ever, the big issue. The state was facing
a deficit of $41 million, but there were plenty of new ways
to spend. The Democrats wanted to increase the base payment for social security from $60 to $65 a month. O'Brien
was advocating state support for kindergartens. Washington was already spending more per public school pupil
than any other state except Delaware; Washington's
$212.12 per pupil was more than twice the U.S. average
of $102.01, and nearly one-third more than California's
$162.29. The new toll road would require $227 million
worth of bonds. The ferry system would require either a
$10-million bond issue or a 30-percent fare increase. Some
people wanted to replace ferry routes with bridges, but a
municipal financing consultant from Chicago told the legislature that current levels of passenger traffic on Puget
Sound would not support construction of a cross-Sound

bridge. Governor Langlie claimed that Eisenhower's tax cuts would save the state $120 million, but no one believed there was any way around raising another $30 to $40 million.

Financial crisis or not, the legislature was too straitlaced to raise money through gambling or sporting events. A bill to establish a state lottery did not pass. A resolution urging the University of Washington Board of Regents to permit a world heavyweight boxing championship match between Rocky Marciano and British fighter Dan Cockrell in the University stadium died in the House on a deadlocked 45 to 45 vote.

The Democrats did not want to raise the sales tax. O'Brien and other Democrats still clung to the idea of a graduated income tax. But that clearly was not in the cards. In the meantime, the state had to pay its bills. In March, fifty of the state's industrial leaders came out against any new type of tax, advocating instead an increase in the existing sales and business taxes.

The legislators wound up doing what they asked, raising the sales tax from 3 to 3 $1/3$ percent. O'Brien and other Democrats who voted for the increase proclaimed that they were "violently opposed in principle to the retrogressive character of this bill," but they concluded that it was "the least objectionable possible at this session." The new Speaker presided over the first sales tax increase since 1941. It was to be only the first of many.

With the tax increase passed, it was clear that the state's budget for the next two years was going to balance. O'Brien pressed Langlie to spend some money on construction at the state institutions. The need was beyond argument, but Langlie would not budge. "While it is likely there will be some excess of income over expenditures for this biennium," he wrote O'Brien, "I am sure you are aware of the fact that the General Fund of the State of Washington is [still] in the red due to the unsound Welfare Initiative 172 [the pension initiative passed by the people in 1948] which was conceived by communist leaders and supported by the Democratic party."

The budget crisis was not the only carryover from the politics of the 1940s. The 1955 legislature wound up dealing with the Canwell Committee, too. The atmosphere in the state and in the nation had changed considerably by then. Although there were still armed conflicts abroad—as the legislature met, communist Chinese troops were shelling the offshore islands of Quemoy and Matsu, held by the Nationalist Chinese—and the country was engaged in the classic cold war with the U.S.S.R., Eisenhower was able to talk of fighting communism not by pulling up the drawbridge but by lowering tariffs, by continuing technical aid to underdeveloped countries, and by granting tax concessions for overseas investment.

Not that the atmosphere had changed totally; when the University of Washington Physics Department recommended the great American physicist J. Robert Oppenheimer as the Walker-Ames lecturer for that year, University President Henry Schmitz announced that Oppenheimer, who had just lost his security clearance because of communist associations in the 1930s, was not welcome. (O'Brien got involved in a minor way. At the request of some University of Washington graduate students, he wrote to Schmitz, asking why Oppenheimer could not lecture at the university. Lest Schmitz think this was a personal crusade, O'Brien explained, "My interest in this matter is only for the purpose of carrying out a request that was made to me.")

Still, the tide had turned against witch hunts. The Army-McCarthy hearings had been held the year before, and Senator Joseph McCarthy, who had conducted anticommunist witch hunts on a national level, had lost his committee chairmanship. He was no longer untouchable. On the fifth day of the legislative session, a headline announced, "SENATE REBUKES MCCARTHY TWICE."

It was time to deal with some excesses of the recent past. The Washington legislature had never revived the Canwell Committee investigations. In 1949, Charles Hodde had had the records of the committee seized and locked away in the capitol. As Hodde recounted it, "Canwell had refused to turn over the records or report back . . . or finish his report to the Legislature, so this arrogant little Speaker [Hodde himself] . . . just sent the State Patrol [and] the sergeant at arms to Canwell's office and . . . brought [the records] down to Olympia; locked them up, saying that we're not going to open them up and embarrass anybody, but we aren't going to leave them out there for him to fiddle around with."

Six years later, however, the legislature still did not know what was in the Canwell Committee's files, and while pressure for a new investigation had waned, neither Canwell nor his approach had been repudiated. During the first part of the 1955 session, someone brought up the fact that the Canwell papers were not really in legislative custody. O'Brien and Lieutenant Governor Emmett Anderson obtained a key from a safe deposit box in an Olympia jewelry store, and—accompanied by FBI agents and the press—they opened the fourth-floor hearing room in which everyone assumed Canwell's records had been stored.

Dust coated everything, even the electrical cords. One metal filing cabinet held a card index with more than 1,000 names, but with no supporting information that would make the names useful. Another held photographs of known communists, a history of Russia for beginners, and some dusty newspapers. There were also three safes to which no one had the combinations. Canwell provided the combination to open one of the safes. The others had to be drilled open by a locksmith. Again with O'Brien, Anderson, and the FBI looking on, the safes were opened. One was completely empty. The second held a transcript of public testimony given at the committee hearings. The third contained some communist literature and a few brief investigative reports.

No significant papers were found. No one knew whether the records found in the House were all that existed, or whether Canwell had a cache of more substantial documents hidden away. Some people speculated that he had given the records to Senator McCarthy. Canwell evidently wanted to encourage the speculation. He would neither deny nor confirm the rumor. "I don't know where they got that idea," was all he said.

O'Brien was incensed. Canwell had deliberately hidden or destroyed documents that belonged to the legislature. O'Brien identified himself with the legislature and its rules. Canwell was setting himself above them.

O'Brien and former Speaker Mort Frayn formed a committee to look into the disappearance of Canwell's records, and the House subpoenaed Canwell to testify at a hearing. The hearing was held in the House chamber on a Monday night with the galleries packed and the state patrol on hand to keep order. As O'Brien remembered it: "We asked Canwell to stay in one of the committee rooms right of the floor until we called him. After we finished questioning him, we put him back in the committee room.

He was a little upset that he couldn't listen to the other testimony. Canwell was kept in isolation because we didn't want to give him a sounding board or let him reply to some of the questions we were asking other people. It was pretty hard for us to keep him under control. A couple of times, when he was sitting right in front of me, I wanted to hit him with the gavel, because I couldn't keep him under control. Canwell would not give us yes or no answers, short answers, without making a speech or a tirade."

When O'Brien asked Canwell about the disappearance of the records, Canwell replied that "if they had fallen into the wrong hands, they might have cost somebody his life." Pressed, Canwell insisted that "they were compiled for my use."

"Do you claim, Al," O'Brien asked, "that the legislature established this committee and appropriated $140,000 [it was actually more than that] just to set you up in business so you could carry on this investigation for your own personal benefit?"

"No," Canwell replied, "it is for the benefit of the state of Washington."

"Then why didn't you turn the records over to the next legislature?" O'Brien demanded. Canwell replied that the next legislature had not been interested.

At one point, O'Brien asked to whom Canwell had given the committee's microfilm. Canwell declined to answer. O'Brien pressed him. Canwell said coyly, "It might be in the hands of an agency whose business is not public."

"Did you give it to the FBI?"

"I decline to answer."

"Are you asking immunity under the Fifth Amendment?" O'Brien asked.

"No," Canwell protested. "Only communists do that."

Two former members of the Canwell Committee testified that the committee had never authorized Canwell to destroy records. Later, in an executive session, Canwell told O'Brien and Frayn that the hearing was part of a campaign against him by the staid *Seattle Times,* which he characterized as a right-wing edition of the communist *Daily Worker.* Describing this testimony later to reporters, O'Brien said, "It was too ridiculous."

The Democratic House talked about citing Canwell for contempt and asked the Republican Attorney General Don Eastvold for his opinion. Eastvold replied that the matter was not in his jurisdiction; the House had to make its own decision. This touched off a sharp exchange.

O'Brien said in early March that "this is a simple case of one Republican trying to help another one who has gotten into trouble. Mr. Eastvold's letter of refusal to act leads me to believe he is acting more as Mr. Canwell's attorney than as the attorney general of the state."

Subsequently, O'Brien said, "I received a letter from the attorney general on the Canwell matter containing more legal double talk. In reply to my last letter, he refers to it as a 'rather old and somewhat confusing political problem.' Actually, the problem is only old in the sense that the activities of the committee took place some six or seven years ago. The actual discovery [by] the state of the records of the Canwell Committee . . . was made only last month. The same can be said of . . . Mr. Canwell's refusal to answer certain questions."

Canwell never did answer. O'Brien and his colleagues never did cite him for contempt. Nonetheless, the spirit of the later 1940s had finally been exorcised. Governor Langlie's war powers bills may or may not have endangered civil liberties, but the Canwell Committee had posed a very real threat, indeed. Until the 1955 hearing, some right-wing legislators had clung to the idea of a new investigation, and there had always been a chance that the rest of the legislature would go along. The hearing made it clear that Canwell had represented no one, that he had taken matters into his own hands, and that his committee had left the legislature with nothing. No one wanted to revive what had obviously been a fiasco. The witch-hunting impulse was not dead in Washington—it would be revived in the early 1960s—but the legislature had had enough.

The 1955 legislature not only laid the ghost of the Canwell Committee once and for all; it almost put an end to another investigative body—the Legislative Council. The council had been formed in 1947 to carry on the legislature's research work in the long intervals between sessions. Originally its task was to study and make recommendations for streamlining the operations of state government. Soon it was able to study anything that the legislature wanted studied. In 1953 the Republican legislature gave it a full-time staff member. Frayn said then that the council should either prove its worth or be abolished. The *Seattle Times* editorialized two years later that it had surely proven its worth.

The Speaker served as chairman of the Legislative Council. In 1953 and 1954, O'Brien served as its vice-chairman. Late in 1954, a council committee chaired by O'Brien recommended the creation of Ways and Means Committees and the introduction of push-button voting. The legislature acted on both recommendations, and when O'Brien became Speaker, he presided over the first House in which they took effect. There would continue to be roll call votes on some issues, but the roll call on every issue—which even O'Brien, with his love of the process, had found tedious—became a thing of the past. Thanks to the Legislative Council, the 1955 legislature also had a modern public address system, and legislative employees were forbidden to lobby. This prohibition, O'Brien said, was meant "to prevent a former practice which has often prevented legislators from pursuing an orderly course of business without constant interruption by employees."

Within the council, O'Brien was said to be working against the recommendation of a merit system for all state employees. Most state jobs were still political appointments, and replacement of patronage with a merit system was an obvious good-government reform. Timing, however, was critical. If a merit system took effect with a Republican administration in power, then all those Republican political appointees would be frozen in office for life. As a Democrat, it was natural for O'Brien to oppose a merit system just then.

Partisanship could obviously creep into the Legislative Council's deliberations. In fact, the council's potential for becoming a partisan tool almost led to its demise. There were twenty-one members, with one party holding a one-vote majority. The Republican Senate wanted twelve members from each party. The Democratic House wanted to keep the numbers at eleven and ten. The final compromise was to keep twenty-one members but to require a two-thirds vote for any investigation or public hearing. That compromise was a long time coming. The wrangling over the Legislative Council lasted through almost the entire session. Because salaries for legislative employees had been linked to council appropriations, the employees had to wait for their paychecks until the legislature was good and ready.

The council did not stay long at death's door. O'Brien helped build it into a robust body with a lot of prestige. During his terms as Speaker, the Legislative Council was often in the limelight. Soon after he gave up the gavel, it became an object of partisan controversy once again.

The council's work included solid background research on issues and legislation, punctuated by hearings that drew considerable public attention. In 1957, after the *Spokane Spokesman-Review* ran an editorial criticizing interim commissions, O'Brien sent the paper a list of the Legislative Council's accomplishments. It had sponsored an urban renewal law; a law that would place the state's medical welfare program under public assistance, which was necessary to get $5 million in federal funds; the consolidation of state land and timber agencies; a law to require building permits; an agricultural marketing act; a law requiring the state to pay school districts on the basis of current, rather than last year's, attendance; and a school district consolidation law. Although O'Brien did not say so, the council in his first year also started laying the groundwork for a state air pollution control law.

In addition, the council involved itself in a less-than-earth-shaking incident that managed to get national attention. In January 1956, University of Washington football coach John Cherberg, who had signed a one-year contract just the month before, was summarily fired. The incident became a minor national *cause célèbre*. *Time* magazine reported in February that "even at the University of Washington, where coaches get fired faster than French premiers, the dismissal of football coach 'Cowboy' Johnny

Cherberg was an unpleasant surprise."

Players had complained in a petition that Cherberg would not let them ride home from games with girls and would not let them whistle in the dressing room, slouch, or chew grass.

In newspaper interviews and on TV, Cherberg said that dissension on the team had been maintained "by threats to players that they would be cut off from outside aid if they joined me . . . A player loyal to me was offered fifty dollars a month . . . from a downtown source to join the movement against me."

Players were getting money from a slush fund run by "Torchy" Torrance, a big University booster who held the printing, food, and beverage concession contracts for all university athletic events. When the trouble over Cherberg began, players who stayed loyal to the coach reportedly stopped getting checks.

The firing of a football coach was an unusual subject for legislative investigation, to say the least, but legislators were not reluctant to enter the glamorous milieu of university football; besides, they could justify investigation on the grounds that the university was a state school, and a Seattle legislator, Republican Richard Rouff, asked the council to take a look. The council talked with the principals at the University of Washington campus on February 6 and 7. On February 7, O'Brien asked Cherberg, "In your opinion, why were you fired?"

Cherberg replied, "The immediate reason was because Mr. Torrance was faced with the possibility of having to give up the fund that he operates." Torrance could throw so much weight around, Cherberg explained, "because the boys were receiving funds, and they were pledged to him." There was no question that the university could, if it wished, fire a football coach who did not win enough games. There *was* a question about the propriety of its contract with Torrance.

O'Brien and the other members of the Legislative Council's executive committee concluded that the university did have authority to fire Cherberg. They also found that legislation might be needed to compel the Associated Students of the University of Washington to call for bids on concessions and purchases over $1,000—and no wonder: a council subcommittee reported in the spring that the school's athletic director personally handed out the concession for printing, and that Torrance's company figured out unilaterally how much money it owed the university as a percentage of its take from the food and beverage concession.

After the dust of the Cherberg firing had settled, O'Brien was approached about running for lieutenant governor. It was a statewide office, but it was largely a figurehead position. "Stub Nelson of the *Seattle Post-Intelligencer* wanted me to run for lieutenant governor," O'Brien said. At the time, "a Catholic nun named Sister Agnes [who administered Providence Hospital in Seattle] was a great personal friend of mine, and I told her one day about people talking to me about the position of lieutenant governor, and all she said to me was, 'John, you don't want that!' And that was it." He decided against abandoning the real influence of the Speakership—and the springboard the Speakership might provide to a more meaningful statewide office. The Democrats wound up running former football coach John Cherberg, instead. Cherberg won. He was to hold the position for the next three decades.

Another Democrat, O'Brien's old 33rd District colleague Albert Rosellini, was elected governor. The 1956 election that brought Rosellini to the governor's mansion gave the Democrats a big majority in the legislature. O'Brien won the caucus vote for Speaker without opposition.

With a Democratic governor in office, the Democratic legislature could draw the boundaries of a new 7th Congressional District without fear of a veto. In April, O'Brien got a "warm note of thanks for the Congressional redistricting law" from Don Magnuson, the Democrat who had been serving, in the absence of a 7th District, as Congressman-at-large. Magnuson said he would be "happy to make a run for it in 1958," and that he was "particularly pleased that the new 7th District takes in the site of the home which I am building."

Drawing up new boundaries for state legislative districts was a much trickier proposition. Despairing of the legislature's willingness to redistrict on its own, the state League of Women Voters had put a redistricting initiative on the ballot in 1956. The League had had to win a court fight just to place redistricting before the voters. It had found that, as the population of Washington grew more urban in the years after World War II, the political imbalance between rural and urban areas had increased dramatically. The League calculated that, according to the 1950 census, an eastern Washington legislator might represent anywhere from 18,000 to 80,000 people; a King County legislator, anywhere from 35,000 to 130,000.

The League's solution, embodied in the initiative, was to redistrict the state, using census tract boundaries as the guidelines. This would have wreaked political havoc. O'Brien would have found himself representing suburban Mercer Island. Individual legislators feared for their seats. The Grange, with its base in the over-represented rural areas, feared for its influence.

Legislators united against the threat. Although they needed two-thirds majorities in both houses, they mustered enough votes to change the initiative into something almost indistinguishable from the status quo.

With redistricting out of the way, the legislature had to deal, as ever, with state finances. By late in the session, budgeted expenditures exceeded revenues by $34 million. O'Brien, who himself had pushed to get extra money for public education, suggested that Rosellini veto both the omnibus budget bill and the supplementary budget bill and call a special session to balance the budget. Rosellini had urged the legislators to finish their business in sixty days. They had done it—O'Brien needed a week to rest up afterward—but neither the governor nor anyone else was pleased by special-interest amendments that had been tacked onto the budget in the last-minute rush. O'Brien pointed out that the House had not even started to act on the appropriations bill until the fifty-ninth day of the session, and he noted that precedents had been set in 1951 and 1955 for dealing with the budget at a special session.

Not all of O'Brien's colleagues were as reluctant as he to accept a budget that handed out so many favors to so many interest groups. "I was astonished to read in yesterday's newspaper where you had advocated that the Governor veto the two budget bills and then call us back immediately into a special session to balance the budget," wrote Clayton Farrington, by then a liberal Democratic legislator from Thurston County, which included Olympia. "This was Langlie's old trick. . . . Most people are

not worried about the budget being out of balance. . . .
The school forces, the PTAs, the state workers, organized
labor, the old people and many others think we did a
wonderful job." Farrington worried that a special session
might make it easier for legislators to cut the something-
for-everyone appropriations than to raise taxes. He wrote,
"John . . . you are a real liberal, a fine Democrat and a
swell guy, but I think on this point, you made a serious
mistake."

The 1957 legislature did not spend all its time dodging
the redistricting initiative and grappling with the budget.
It also passed some laws with lasting results. One law allowed public utilities to create the Washington Public Power
Supply System (WPPSS). Public power wanted the law so
that PUDs could jointly build generating plants. The legislation attracted virtually no attention. O'Brien voted for
it without a second thought. WPPSS later became nation-
ally notorious for trying and failing to build five nuclear
plants at once, a quixotic undertaking that ultimately forced
it to default on $2.25 billion worth of bonds.

Another law, arousing more controversy at the time but
occasioning fewer second thoughts, permitted the creation of Metro—the Municipality of Metropolitan Seattle.
This amalgamation of Seattle and suburban sewer districts was to reverse the growing pollution of Lake Washington and was eventually to take over public transportation in King County. Largely the brainchild of Seattle
bond attorney James Ellis, Metro had the support of both
the League of Women Voters and the Municipal League,
but it also had a lot of opposition. Conservatives from south
Snohomish County, north of Seattle, did not want to get
enmeshed with urban King County or its problems. Sub-
urbanites worried that the new municipality would force

them to deal with urban problems they had hoped to escape by moving to the suburbs. Engineering firms that represented existing sewer districts feared that if Metro started planning all the sewers, they would lose work. Party politicians worried that a nonpartisan organization with power over major public works projects would dilute their opportunities for patronage.

The enabling legislation took a long time getting through the senate, and it arrived in the House—where one of its floor leaders was a freshman legislator named Dan Evans—with very little time left in the session. James Ellis, who was lobbying for the bill, would be there waiting every day when O'Brien left the rostrum, to see how it was going.

It almost went very badly. The bill was referred to the Cities and Counties Committee chaired by Wally Carmichael, who represented Mountlake Terrace, in Snohomish County. Mountlake Terrace was just developing and feared Metro might restrict its ability to deal with sewage as it pleased. Sentiment ran against the proposed municipality. Carmichael reflected the views of his constituency. He announced that he was not going to let the bill out of committee.

Carmichael "was just sitting on it," O'Brien recalled. "He was going to kill it. Mountlake Terrace was in his legislative district, and people in Mountlake Terrace didn't want it. People in Renton, Kent, and Auburn didn't want it, either."

James Ellis was alarmed. As he recalled years later, "Floyd Miller [a former legislator and later Seattle City Councilman who was working for the bill] and I went down to John [who said,] 'Well, we'll see about that.'" O'Brien called Carmichael to his office and, in Ellis's words, "read Carmichael the riot act." As Ellis remembered it, Carmichael

said, "I'm running this committee, and I'm not going to
do this."

O'Brien replied, "Well, I'm running this House."

"One day," O'Brien said later, "I told him that if he
didn't call a meeting and act on the bill favorably, I was
going to go up to his committee and call a meeting for
him. So he did. He called a meeting, and the committee
reported the bill to the House. Then it was placed on the
calendar of the House for consideration. A lot of people
from south King County were very much opposed to the
Metro bill. Many legislators said afterward the only reason that bill was passed was that I wanted it."

(The final vote could not have been closer. The whole
Snohomish County delegation was opposed. One Snohomish County legislator, Paul Stocker, had a pet bill bottled up in the Commerce Committee, chaired by O'Brien's
close friend Ray Olsen. Olsen offered Stocker a deal: if
the man from Snohomish County would arrange to leave
the floor for a telephone call at the time the vote was taken
on Metro—so he would not be there to vote no—Olsen
would let his bill out of committee. Stocker agreed. He
had the sergeant at arms summon him to the phone right
before the crucial vote. He left. The Metro bill passed by
exactly one vote. True to his word, Olsen then let Stocker's bill out of committee, but it was subsequently killed.)

Other legislation passed in 1957 set the stage for Century 21, the Seattle World's Fair. The 1955 legislature had
set up a commission to study the feasibility of a fair. The
legislators of 1957 decided that the fair would be in Seattle, established a nonprofit corporation to run it, and—
most important—authorized $7.5 million in state bonds
to help pay for it.

The next year, O'Brien and his wife Mary went to Belgium with the Rosellinis to check out the Brussels World's Fair. When O'Brien returned in June, he reported to the Legislative Council. "One significant happening has occurred at Brussels which needs the consideration of the Legislative Council and the World's Fair Commission," he said. "The complaints of tourists were so bitter on the high prices for food and lodging that the merchants had to cut their prices. In some instances, the prices were still very high. Fountain service at the American pavilion was at least 100 percent higher than what is charged locally.

"The Legislative Council might consider recommending to the legislature that standby price-control legislation be enacted to warn the unscrupulous operator. Or perhaps the World's Fair Commission could work out a gentleman's agreement with the food and lodging industry to control prices, so that this sort of thing could not happen here."

The Legislative Council reimbursed O'Brien for half of his round-trip ticket to Brussels; payment for the other half—$562.85—was disallowed by State Auditor Cliff Yelle. Yelle refused to acknowledge the trip as reimbursable state business. "Apparently," O'Brien wrote to Yelle, "you have done everything possible to embarrass me on my official visit to the Brussels World's Fair." Yelle denied this. But he would not budge.

This was not the first trouble O'Brien had had with Yelle that year. The House had voted to pay O'Brien $400 a month for performing his duties as Speaker, in addition to his regular $100 monthly legislative salary. But Yelle had included the Speaker's stipend in a citizens' lawsuit challenging the payment of per diem expense money to state officials living in Olympia. Because the stipend had been approved by only one house, the state supreme court ruled that it was illegal. O'Brien could be reimbursed for his actual expenses between sessions, but the balance of the money had to be repaid.

There was no suggestion of impropriety. Decades later, some legislators would marvel at the fact that people were still expected to assume the time-consuming duties of Speaker without any extra compensation. O'Brien made some enemies during his years as Speaker, but he was never accused of using the position to feather his own nest. Unassailably honest himself, he was quick to defend the sometimes questionable propriety of his fellow legislators. In late 1957, Rosellini's legal adviser, George Kahin, asked the Legislative Council to investigate legislators' personal interests in legislation. O'Brien asked Kahin to name one occasion during the 1957 session in which a legislator had had a direct financial interest in a bill. Kahin said that when he was the governor's advisor, such conflicts of interest were discussed around the capitol all the time. He had not heard any names mentioned, but the situation was clearly a scandal. "To check such stories does not warrant an investigation," O'Brien replied. "We try to conduct ourselves on a very high plane."

(O'Brien was not the only legislator who waxed indignant over Kahin's charges. The Republican floor leader, Lincoln Shropshire, wrote O'Brien that "in my personal opinion, the legislators on the Republican side of the aisle will and do resent the implications of Mr. Kahin's statements." A Wapato Republican, Cecil C. Clark, wrote to him that "this statement of Mr. George Kahin that 60 percent to 80 percent of the members of the Legislature received retainers from private interests is quite disconcerting. It casts a shadow of suspicion on the whole Legislature. Are you in the 60 to 80 percent? I'm not.")

O'Brien and the rest of the council's executive committee turned Kahin down.

The council did take a look—another look—at the idea of a merit system. An estimated 5,000 state jobs had changed hands in the first year of the Rosellini administration, so the Democratic legislature would not have had to freeze all those Republican officeholders in place, but the idea was still controversial. A merit system would have to wait for a different year.

The 1958 election went Democratic again, with O'Brien getting 20 percent more votes than the other Democrat in his district, more than three times as many votes as the only Republican. Once again, he won his party's nomination for Speaker without opposition.

His prestige was at a pinnacle. His old patron Ed Reilly had also served three terms as Speaker, but no one had ever won the job more times than that. When then Senator John F. Kennedy came to town for a Jefferson–Jackson Day Dinner, O'Brien was one of his hosts.

Democrats were looking for someone to oppose Republican Gordon Clinton for mayor of Seattle. O'Brien was approached as a possible candidate. The King County Democratic Central Committee urged him to run. The vice-chairman of the 31st Precinct Committeemen's Organization wrote him: "We . . . are sincerely hoping that you will decide to be the Mayor of Seattle next term. Much too long we have watched this growing city stymied by indecision [and] conservative inaction and [we] would welcome a change."

O'Brien was giving serious consideration to running for mayor but, according to Ross Cunningham's report in the

Seattle Times, he was going to take a survey before he made any decision. There was no question about his abilities. The year before Rosellini was elected governor, a group of state Democratic officials, meeting on the top floor of the Chinook Hotel in Yakima, took an informal vote on which Democrat was the best man for the governorship— not who was most electable or most desirable for other reasons; just who was the best man. O'Brien won, hands down.

"He was the greatest Speaker we ever had around here," Ed Munro, who was chairman of the King County Democrats at the time, said later. "He would have made a good mayor." But O'Brien was not sure he wanted to run for mayor of Seattle. "I ran into [former] Mayor [Allan] Pomeroy one time on the streets," O'Brien recalled, "and he asked me, 'Why do you want to run for mayor?' " O'Brien did not have a good answer. "He wasn't too steamed up about taking that job," Munro said. He also was not sure he could win. "It would have been sort of a gamble," he figured, and he did not want to take the risk.

"He could have been mayor," Munro insisted, but when a group of Democratic leaders met with him in downtown Seattle to talk about running, he "told the group that met with him . . . jesus!" Munro exclaimed. "He wanted $25,000 on the line [for campaign expenses] before he filed!" At that point, people simply did not give money to candidates before they filed. O'Brien had set a condition that was not likely to be met. At the end of 1959, he told his would-be supporters that he was not a candidate.

Instead of campaigning for the mayor's office, O'Brien ran again for the House in 1960. The Municipal League lauded his "outstanding performance as a legislator." He won easily, getting half again as many votes as both his district's Republicans combined. Rosellini won a second term as governor. John F. Kennedy won the presidency. The Eisenhower era was over. In Washington State, the Democrats again controlled the House. Nothing seemed to stand in the way of an unprecedented fourth term as Speaker for John O'Brien.

V

Saving the Day for Public Power

O'BRIEN HAD A DEMOCRATIC MAJORITY AND A LOT OF prestige, but his days of clear sailing to the Speakership were over. Things had changed. It was not simply that the Kennedy 1960s were going to be very different from the Eisenhower 1950s. Events were making O'Brien's hold less secure. His powerful ally, Julia Butler Hansen, had moved on to Congress. Ambitious younger men in the House were ready to make their own bids for power. Private utilities had started spending more money and pulling more strings in their effort to gain an advantage over the PUDs. It was no secret that private power had given money to Democratic candidates in the 1960 election, and that O'Brien was not private power's choice for Speaker.

O'Brien's main rival for the Speakership was a young lawyer from Puyallup, east of Tacoma, named Leonard Sawyer. Sawyer, whose local prestige as a former high school athlete had helped him get elected, was unquestionably able. But some people who knew him at various stages of his legislative career also felt that something was not quite right. He was never caught doing anything illegal, but there was always, in some people's minds, a question of impropriety. Ken Billington, then head of the state PUD association and lobbyist for the PUDs in Olympia, has described Sawyer "driving his white T-bird all over the state" giving out private power money for local races. Herb Legg, then state Democratic chairman, has characterized the 1961 session as one "in which money was fairly decisive."

One of Sawyer's allies was Representative August Mardesich, another up-and-coming Democratic legislator. Mardesich "was a basic public power supporter and later was very positive in helping me," Ken Billington has written, "but for this particular session, he was cooperating with those supporting private power on strategy votes and House organizing."

Another Sawyer ally was second-term Seattle legislator Robert (Bob) Perry. Perry was a bright, aggressive union business agent. Even people who later disapproved heartily of things he had done found him pleasant and interesting. Perry took money from Washington Water Power to get reelected in 1960, according to his own testimony years later, and he actually went onto the payroll of a Washington Water Power subsidiary, the Washington Irrigation and Development Corporation, around that time. "Did you consider that as a payoff for your political work?" Perry was asked before a federal grand jury in 1981. He replied, "At the time . . . I didn't have a job. I couldn't stay in politics and get a job because I would have had to be a building tradesman or some other thing. . . . When I [was elected] they put me on the payroll as they did several other legislators."

Bob Perry's involvement with Washington Water Power eventually led him to jail. O'Brien considered his fellow Seattle legislator somewhat mysterious. "Nobody knew too much about him," O'Brien said later. "He was supposed to have been from Hollywood, and his father was a well-known musician, and he had a labor background and was close to private power people."

Perry himself told the grand jury, "I never told anybody I worked for [a Washington Water Power subsidiary], either. It was on my income tax form, but I never told any of the legislators." Perry made it clear to the grand jury that Washington Water Power's attempts to influence legislation would not necessarily show up on an income tax return or a legitimate campaign disclosure form. He was asked, "Did [Washington Water Power vice-president and lobbyist Jeremiah] Buckley ever come and give you undisclosed money under the table?"

He replied, "Over the years, yes."

"How was the money given?"

"In cash, in white envelopes."

O'Brien was overconfident going into the Democratic caucus at which a Speaker would be chosen. Sawyer and Mardesich had worked hard at lining up votes. They had gotten their troops together right after the September primary. After the November election, their group had met in a Seattle hotel restaurant and decided to back Sawyer for Speaker. There were enough of them to pull it off.

And they had help. "Si Holcomb, the chief clerk, was sort of upset with me," O'Brien recalled, "and he was guiding them." The friction between Holcomb and O'Brien was not strictly political. "In the '59 session," O'Brien said, "he wasn't even around for the closing ceremonies. I think he was gone for about a month. He was holed up in a motel room someplace." O'Brien was not willing to turn a blind eye. "I proceeded to take him off the payroll. The staff didn't think he should be paid and I just took him off. I didn't have much choice, but he never forgot that. I had that happen to me in other instances, too, where maybe I saw people doing things that I didn't subscribe to, and when I opposed [them], they didn't like it."

On the first ballot, O'Brien, who had won his two previous terms unopposed, found himself tied with Sawyer, 29 to 29. The second ballot, too, was a dead heat. Sawyer said afterward that if Representative Clayton Farrington had not gone to Arizona for his arthritis, the insurgents would have had the extra vote they needed to win. But Farrington was out of town, and Sawyer had gone as far as he could go.

"That was when Perry started his strong-arm tactics," O'Brien recalled. "Bob comes up to me in the caucus and says to me, 'We're going to get you the next vote. We're going to get you.'"

But they did not. On the third ballot, the insurgents ran Augie Mardesich for Speaker. By then, O'Brien had had time to talk with some of the people voting against him. The deadlock was broken. The night before the legislative session started, O'Brien had dinner with Sawyer and Mardesich. Mardesich joked about the Last Supper. The next day, when the session began, O'Brien's mother was in the gallery to see him become the first man ever to win the Speakership four times.

O'Brien's election did not end the tension. He gave all the committee chairmanships to Democrats who had supported him. One of the legislators who had helped swing the election to O'Brien was John Goldmark, a rancher and attorney from Okanogan, in sparsely populated north-central Washington. Goldmark was the leader of the young liberal House Democrats who had served in World War II and were just getting elected to state office. They would get together every night to go over legislation that was going to come up the following day. A member of the group, Frank Brouillet, who had been elected in 1957, recalled that "some of us were not willing to accept" the autocratic way the House was run. "We didn't trust what the leaders told us. We used to sit up all night and read all the bills." They were among the best-informed members of the House. O'Brien was not part of their circle. During the late 1950s, "he used to send me to find out what some of the young liberals were thinking," Julia Butler Hansen said. "He didn't have much conversation with them."

But they could make common cause. Goldmark himself went into the caucus as a candidate for Speaker. He was not a serious contender; the real contest was between O'Brien and Sawyer. Seeing how things stood, Goldmark withdrew, giving his support—and his supporters—to O'Brien. If Goldmark had not pulled a few votes out of the Sawyer camp, O'Brien would have lost on the first round.

After Goldmark helped him win, O'Brien took the chairmanship of the powerful Ways and Means Committee away from Mardesich and gave it to Goldmark. He named Mardesich assistant Speaker pro tem. Mardesich said, "I never heard of it before. I don't know what it is." There was talk of the dissident Democrats forming a coalition with the Republicans. Perry was evidently all for this—and was angry with Sawyer when Sawyer refused to go along.

Dissidents claimed O'Brien had reneged on promises about committee assignments. They said he had promised them two of four key committee chairmanships and a chance to pick four members of the Rules Committee.

O'Brien replied that four of their members were already on Rules and that his giving the chairmanship of the Utilities Committee to Dick Kink of Bellingham, ninety miles north of Seattle—who had worked for Puget Power since the previous session—had been a major concession.

Sawyer said, "O'Brien did not come close to keeping his commitments." O'Brien replied, "[The dissidents] say I did not keep my commitments, and I say they did not keep their commitments to the Democratic party." The Republican floor leader, Dan Evans, sided with O'Brien, saying, "He has been fair."

The fight within the House quickly gave way to a fight between the House and the governor. Rosellini asked the legislature for $57.8 million in new taxes to balance the budget, with most of the additional money going to the public schools, some of it to increase teachers' salaries. Evans introduced a resolution that asked the governor to furnish some messy details: either specific budget cuts or specific new taxes to pay for the budget he had introduced. The Republicans did not have enough votes to carry the resolution by themselves, but they were joined by Mardesich and some of the other Democrats who had supported Sawyer. The resolution passed.

O'Brien quickly called the Democrats into a caucus. The troops were rebellious. One allegedly said, "There will not be any tax increase out of this legislature if we have to stay here until September." Another said it was "time we told the school forces that they have gone too far. They want too much and it is impossible to satisfy them. The school budget has to be cut." The caucus lasted over an hour. Then it sent a delegation including O'Brien, Sawyer, and Mardesich to talk with Governor Rosellini. The late afternoon meeting turned out to be "a shouting, bitter session."

The next day, O'Brien called another caucus. He told the Democrats that Rosellini would not recommend specific tax increases, but he would work with the Democratic leaders to develop recommendations—if yesterday's resolution was voted down. It was. Mardesich and Sawyer went along with the rest of their party, and the Democrats, with only two of their members dissenting, killed the resolution on a straight party-line vote.

Rosellini's troubles with the legislature were not over. He brought the next problem on himself. Only days after the Republican resolution was killed, Rosellini introduced a bill that would have enabled him to appoint a new State Liquor Control Board. A 1948 initiative had set the terms of liquor board members at nine years. This will was designed to change the ground rules entirely. Rosellini would be able to get rid of the board's chairman, Don Abel, and another member whom he had not appointed, and to name new members who would serve at his pleasure.

Ross Cunningham broke the story in the *Seattle Times*. Cunningham had been alerted to the governor's plans when Abel called him, very upset, from Olympia, and drove up to Seattle for a talk. Abel feared that the Colacurccios—tavern and nightclub owners with widely suspected ties to organized crime—were going to be given control of liquor licensing. Abel wanted no part of it, he said, so he was on his way out.

Rosellini had long been considered close to liquor interests. The 1955 directory of state legislators said he was "reputed to have tavern owners in his camp." When he was governor, some of the men who made big money selling liquor to the state went around with little roses in their lapels to show they were Rosellini supporters.

The liquor board bill was introduced in the Senate earlier than had been expected and was rammed through in five minutes. That left it up to the House. It stayed there for weeks, with other bills held hostage until it passed. On March 3, Representative Damon Canfield of Granger, in south-central Washington, explained, "Word reached members of the House today to pass the liquor board bill or face trouble at home by having education bills locked up in committee."

Dan Evans said, "The governor and his team are keeping education bills in the deep freeze, with the governor's pet bill, giving him control of the liquor board, as the price for thawing out education measures."

O'Brien replied that the charges were "completely false, ridiculous and amateurish."

They were not. O'Brien steered a course that some might call cautious but that some considered courageous. He did not publicly turn against the governor on the liquor board bill. In February, when Representative Wes Uhlman, later mayor of Seattle, moved that the bill be sent to his Committee on Higher Education for study, instead of to the Liquor Control Committee—a move that would have killed it—O'Brien said, "I refuse to recognize you for that purpose." In March, when Eric Braun of Cashmere moved that the bill be postponed indefinitely, O'Brien told him that unless a bill coming from committee had two-thirds against it, it went automatically to Rules.

But O'Brien did not push the bill, either, despite not-so-subtle pressure to do so. Rosellini's "friends called me from all over the country," he recalled. Men in Chicago, Palm Springs, and elsewhere urged him to take a more active role. He refused. Payton Smith, the Speaker's attorney for the 1961 session, remembered that cases of whiskey were being dispensed liberally while the liquor bill was pending. At one point, the governor left a message that a case of a certain kind of whiskey was waiting at a certain place. O'Brien just said, "We'd better leave it there." Another time, the governor called on the phone, saying he wanted to talk with O'Brien right away. O'Brien would not talk to him. O'Brien's conduct in the liquor board fight convinced Ross Cunningham—who covered state politics for half a century—that he had character.

When the bill reached the floor, the gallery was full of liquor vendors. The ensuing debate was punctuated by cheers and boos and enlivened by the spectacle of O'Brien threatening to have Dan Evans thrown out. O'Brien said at one point that the House should keep the debate on a high plane. Evans cracked, "I think we can keep debate on a high plane, even if this is a low bill." O'Brien banged his gavel and told Evans to sit down if he did not want to be ejected.

The debate lasted more than three hours. It ended late at night when the House approved a compromise devised by O'Brien and introduced by assistant Democratic floor leader Bob Schaefer: all members of the liquor board appointed before January 15 could serve out their current terms; any new members would be appointed for five years instead of seven. The original bill was referred back to committee. O'Brien thought "some Democrats looked like the world had ended."

O'Brien rationalized that he had given up on the governor's bill because it obviously was not going to pass. He had given it a fair shot, but the votes just were not there. The truth was that he had not tried very hard. It was also true that the Republicans were ready to filibuster, and by that stage of the session, no one had the stomach for another filibuster.

(The liquor board was not the only beverage issue in 1961. Charles Hodde, by then the governor's director of revenue, had advocated a tax on soft drinks. Rosellini, considered close to soft drink distributors as well as liquor interests, had opposed it. Rosellini had said he would not veto a soft drink tax if it passed. A tax bill was introduced. When the bill reached the floor of the House, the galleries were packed with representatives of soft drink companies. The House was deadlocked, 49 to 49. O'Brien cast the deciding vote in favor of the tax. Rosellini vetoed it after all.)

The longest filibuster in state history had taken place a few weeks before. It was the dramatic high point of the session, of the decades-long fight between private and public power, and, very likely, of John O'Brien's legislative career.

Private power was pushing a bill, House Bill 197, that would have required a vote of the people before a PUD could condemn private utility property. The immediate issue was an attempt by the Thurston County PUD to take over part of the Puget Power system. Polls convinced Puget Power that a majority of the people in Thurston County opposed a takeover, but the PUD seemed determined. The broader issue was the same as it had always been.

Republicans by and large backed private power. Democrats by and large backed the PUDs, but most Democrats from Spokane were sympathetic—and, many people assumed, beholden—to Washington Water Power.

The bill's first stop was the Public Utilities Committee, chaired by private power sympathizer Dick Kink. The committee's members included Washington Water Power agent Bob Perry, Spokane Democrats Margaret Hurley and William Day, and Dan Evans, all of whom could be counted on to take private power's side. The bill made it through that committee on a vote of 13 to 12, then went to Rules, where its passage seemed highly uncertain.

Some public power supporters on the Rules Committee assumed they had half the committee's votes, enough to keep the bill from reaching the floor. They were wrong. They had not realized that some legislators would play both sides, identifying with public power but, when given a chance to vote in secret, casting their ballots for the other side. The PUD Association's Ken Billington, who was lobbying against the bill, learned this political fact at a reception at the Benson Hotel in Portland, Oregon. George Brunzell, president of Washington Water Power, was there, and during the evening, the two political rivals chatted. Billington was surprised when Brunzell "said they had two 'labor' votes on the House Rules Committee and could 'pull' HB 197 any time they wanted. I found out after that he was absolutely correct . . . When I returned to Olympia the following Monday, I checked with Speaker O'Brien. . . . He made no comment but did inform me that by a previous pledge to Representative Hurley, he had to allow a secret ballot on HB 197 in the Rules Committee." On a secret ballot, private power did have those two votes. The bill passed the Rules Committee 11 to 7.

The public power forces knew they did not have enough votes to kill the bill on the floor of the House. They needed fifty. They started with little more than forty votes and couldn't get beyond forty-nine. Democrat Clayton Farrington, who might have provided the fiftieth vote, had been sick. He had also been under a lot of political pressure in his Thurston County district because of the fight between the Thurston County PUD and Puget Power. During roll-call votes, he was repeatedly absent.

Without a majority, the public power forces decided to stall until they could win over someone from the opposition. They would never have been able to pull it off without a capable and highly partisan Speaker on their side. They had one. Billington has written that "probably the greatest strength in the issue came from Speaker John O'Brien, who was still smarting under the attempt by the pro-private power Democrats to unseat him."

"The first day of the filibuster the private power Democrats all started taking their coats off," O'Brien recalled years later. They were "going to show me. Bill McCormick took his coat off on the floor of the House; so I said right from the rostrum, 'Mr. McCormick, put your coat back on!' I probably shouldn't have done that; I probably should have sent a page. He never forgot that, either. He felt I had embarrassed him. So they put their coats back on. That's how the feeling ran in the House."

The first day of debate set the tone. "The right-to-vote slogan is essentially a fraud," John Goldmark said. "This is nothing more than a gimmick to throw a roadblock into the way of public power development."

"Not so," replied Ed Harris of Spokane. "To deny the right to vote is to deny the people's right to home rule."

Shirley Marsh of Longview, on the Columbia River, in PUD territory, said the people had already had a chance to vote by electing PUD commissioners.

Harry Lewis disagreed, insisting that "the keystone of democracy is the right to vote."

Democratic floor leader Mark Litchman said he was all for the right to vote, but "this is probably one of the worst and most vicious bills ever to come before the House. Its purpose is to curtail development of public power."

"Let's not get our wires crossed," retorted Margaret Hurley. "The people who oppose this bill are against the people's right to vote. Are we afraid of what they are going to do when they get the right to vote?"

What the public power establishment still feared was that private power would basically be able to buy votes. But Harry Lewis pointed out that the PUDs were not exactly helpless. "In 1958–59 our PUD paid $12,000 to the Washington Public Utility District Commissioners Association," he said, "and it is recognized as one of the most powerful lobby groups here."

The Democratic floor leaders tried to get a thirty-minute recess so they would have time to build up their forces. Their motion was voted down. Another delaying move was defeated. Then a public power Democrat moved that the bill be indefinitely postponed. That started a debate that lasted until lunchtime. The mood in the House was so antagonistic that the motion to break for lunch carried by only two votes.

The public power side kept introducing amendments and procedural motions, demanding a time-consuming roll-call vote on everything. O'Brien recognized every delaying motion. Nothing was out of order or not germane.

The debate continued. The public power forces lost some thirty roll-call votes on amendments and motions that would have buried the bill in committee.

But they were eating up the clock. And they had reportedly stockpiled more than 200 amendments for future use. The barrage of motions, amendments, and impassioned speeches continued into the night.

Around seven o'clock, the public power forces wanted

to cut things off for the day. The private power legislators did not want to let them do so. Ken Billington has written that "it became obvious to Speaker O'Brien by 7:00 P.M. that tempers were flaring and order in the chamber might not be maintained." O'Brien himself recalled that "we had a member named Horace Bozarth from [the central Washington apple-growing city of] Wenatchee [actually, from nearby Mansfield], a member of the Grange who had a real feeling about this private versus public power issue. He was suffering from pains in the back of his neck and the blood vessels in his eyes, and I thought he was going to pass out on me, but he wouldn't leave and we couldn't get him excused. They wouldn't let him leave. We had tried. We had two doctors who both moved that Horace Bozarth be excused from the call of the House. The House wouldn't let him do it. But at seven o'clock or seven-thirty I had the floor leader give me two fast motions: a move to dispense with the call of the House and a move to adjourn. He was a little slow, but I put the motions fast and said: 'The ayes have it; the House is adjourned.' I came down with the gavel; the papers, pencils, and pad on the lectern flew up; and I left. Some of the members were yelling out on the floor of the House."

The ayes clearly did not have it—or would not have had it if O'Brien had not been so quick with his gavel and so firm in his determination to wrap things up. Republicans and private power Democrats were outraged. Payton Smith recalled, "That was the only time I ever saw Dan Evans lose his cool."

Republicans were waving their arms and shouting, trying to force O'Brien to recognize them. He would not. He just walked out. The shouting continued.

Ken Billington felt there might be physical violence. O'Brien felt the same. "I was going to call the state patrol to get me out," he said later. "Then Representative Dick Taylor came in—a big former basketball star from Stanford University, six foot eight, a huge person. He came in and it was all over."

O'Brien had "lost control not only of the House but of himself," Evans said after the House adjourned. "The Speaker . . . absolutely abdicated his responsibility to members of the House to conduct our affairs according to long-established rule. . . . The actions today were a flagrant example of rule by a minority over the wishes of a clear majority."

Republican Cecil Clark said, "Stalin couldn't have done any better in thwarting the right of the majority."

"The next day," O'Brien recalled, "they still had kind of a feeling, but afterward, we carried on a pretty orderly debate." There was another barrage of delaying tactics, with one trivial amendment or procedural motion following another. Sometimes the public power legislators would sneak out of the chamber; debate would be held up until the sergeant at arms could find them and bring them back. Wes Uhlman was found at the top of the steps in the capitol dome.

The amendments and motions did not come out of thin air. A group of legislators met every night to get them ready for the next day. "John Goldmark was one of the main participants," O'Brien said. "John worked every night along with four or five others, preparing amendments for the next day."

On the third day of the filibuster, Bruce Burns of Tacoma accused private power of payoffs, but so many charges had already been thrown around that no one paid any attention. The state's Democratic political heavy-weights, Senators Jackson and Magnuson, sent O'Brien a telegram expressing their opposition to House Bill 197. But nothing changed. The debate lasted until 12:35 A.M.

On the morning of the fourth day, one of the bill's original sponsors, Avery Garrett of Seattle, moved to re-refer it to the Rules Committee. During the lunch recess a Republican from a PUD county, Merrill Folsom, who had supported the bill consistently, found Ken Billington in "ulcer gulch," where the lobbyists hung out. Folsom told Billington he had been assured that the two sides would eventually work out a compromise. Billington replied that there could be no compromise. Folsom went back prepared to vote for the motion to re-refer.

The motion carried, 51 to 47. Dan Evans voted for it. He said he thought he was voting no. Some people figured he just wanted to be in a position to move for reconsideration, which he could do only if he had been part of the majority. O'Brien's gavel was much too quick, though, to permit any motion to reconsider. House Bill 197 went back to the Rules Committee. The great filibuster of 1961 was over.

Lingering bitterness from the power fight and the earlier fight over the Speakership would soon have repercussions both for O'Brien and the Democratic party. "The private power people were very bitter toward John," Frank Brouillet observed. "John was kind of a four-letter word for them." The opponents did not fold their tents and slip away. Leonard Sawyer told the Pierce County Men's Democratic Luncheon Club in May that "there was a little lack of leadership in the front row. . . . All the floor leaders never had been leaders before. This created a bad image. John should have worked on merit rather than pressure. John did a good job as Speaker, but it was embarrassing when he had to send notes down to his leaders to tell them what to do and what motions to make."

Perry was dismissed from his job as a union business agent. Now, he would depend more than ever on Washington Water Power.

All of this meant trouble for O'Brien in the long run. In the short run, the 1961 session enhanced his stature. O'Brien read a lot of articles that talked about those two outstanding legislative leaders, Dan Evans and John O'Brien. People started to discuss both men as potential candidates for governor.

VI

Brought Down
by Strange Bedfellows

O'BRIEN WAS AT THE CENTER OF THINGS. THAT SUM-
mer, when the National Conference of State Legislative
Leaders met in Nevada. O'Brien, by then a member of
the executive committee, persuaded the group to sched-
ule its 1962 meeting at Seattle's Olympic Hotel. O'Brien
liked associating with legislative leaders from around the
country. It was, perhaps, a substitute for holding a higher
office. It meant a lot to him that when the Century 21
World's Fair was in full swing, they would be meeting in
his hometown.

The Legislative Council, of which he was still chairman,
had been very much in the limelight. In January, newly
elected Seattle Port Commissioner Gordon Newell had
asked for a legislative investigation of the port. Newell
claimed that management of the port was very loose. There
were questions about personal expenses, about club mem-
berships paid for with public money, about the adequacy
of financial returns on leased land.

In July, the council held a televised hearing on the
management of the port. The information that came out
was, if not damning, unlikely to inspire public trust. "About
the greasing of the purchasing agent's palm," O'Brien asked

Port Commissioner Tom McManus, "do you have any knowledge of specific incidents, or is this just a rumor?"

"No sir," McManus replied, "I do not. This is what I had been told by salesmen that had been doing business with the port. That a case of whiskey helped . . . or a box of cigars or some such—in other words, sort of a necessary calling card."

Another time, O'Brien asked McManus, "How many of the staff use port vehicles on weekends?"

McManus answered, "Every car at the Port of Seattle is used."

In addition to the petty improprieties, there were serious allegations of financial ineptitude. Newell noted that although the port had just handled its greatest volume of peacetime cargo ever, it had lost money. The Municipal League had reported that fourteen of the port's thirty-eight operations were in the red.

O'Brien wondered about wasteful competition among Puget Sound ports, a subject that was to interest him on and off for many years. "Is there much cut-throat competition between Tacoma and Everett and Seattle?" he asked.

"Very little," Port Commissioner C. H. Carlander replied.

"Then it won't be necessary for us to recommend a Puget Sound Port Authority or a Washington State Port Authority," O'Brien said. He was to reconsider that opinion before the end of the decade.

The Legislative Council turned up nothing scandalous about the Port of Seattle. It did make a series of recommendations, not least that the port have a strong executive director and that port commissioners keep their noses out of day-to-day administration.

The next year, the Legislative Council looked into alleged price gouging and evictions by Seattle landlords who wanted to get long-term tenants out of the way so they could make a killing from visitors to the world's fair. O'Brien had warned about price gouging, when he reported on the Brussels World's Fair. In 1961, the Seattle City Council had passed an ordinance that authorized the granting of licenses to landlords who wanted to change apartment buildings to hotels despite building and zoning codes. Tenants were evicted, and there was a public outcry. The council repealed the ordinance at the beginning of 1962. The twenty-one people who held licenses to convert their apartment buildings to hotels were asked to give them back. Only three did.

"The legislature appropriated $10.5 million to set up a world's fair for the benefit of everyone in Seattle and the state, not to cause undue hardship on the people living here," O'Brien said. "We didn't foresee price gouging and evictions." But angry tenants claimed that was exactly what had happened. City officials claimed they had no power to stop the landlords. Two city councilmen-elect, Wing Luke and Lud Kramer, called for a joint meeting of city and state officials to work out a solution. Seattle attorney William Dwyer told a group of tenants, though, that the city council could pass any number of ordinances to solve the problem.

A week later, the Legislative Council sent mimeographed questionnaires about Century 21 housing to Seattle apartment managers and owners, some of whom had clearly thrown people out to make room for a higher-paying clientele. The Showboat Apartments at 3711 15th Avenue N.E., for example, had twenty-five units available for Century 21 visitors—the result of twenty-five evictions. The Council concluded that although abuses were scattered rather than citywide, they certainly existed.

And the abuses were getting a lot of press. Ralph L. Lee, director of Expo-Lodging, the world's fair lodging agency, said that "the publicity about evictions is becoming widespread throughout the United States, probably deterring a lot of fair visitors from coming into the area."

Before an audience of irate tenants on April 4, the Seattle City Council voted to revoke the eighteen outstanding licenses permitting apartment owners to convert their buildings to hotels. But the attorney for the Seattle Renters' Association said that those eighteen licenses were merely the tip of the iceberg: she had a list of 130 apartment houses from which Seattle residents had been evicted to make room for visitors to the fair. When Lieutenant Governor John Cherberg suggested that Expo-Lodging help the evicted tenants find homes, he drew applause. When Mayor Gordon Clinton asked people not to applaud, he was booed.

Some people thought the legislature should hold a special session to deal with the evictions. O'Brien was not among them. He explained that state intervention "would make headlines all over the country. Everything we have done would be in jeopardy. We must do everything possible before we go the route of a special session."

No special session was held. Problems got ironed out. The fair was a great success. In June, the National Conference of State Legislative Leaders descended on the Olympic Hotel. O'Brien was named to the group's executive committee.

He was still riding high. But before June ended, he had to turn his attention from the pleasant ceremonies of a national conference and a world's fair to the unpleasant realities of state politics.

The state Democratic convention was held in late June in Bellingham. It was clear from the beginning that O'Brien and his supporters might be in for trouble. Resentments aroused by the power bill fight were still simmering. State Democratic Chairman Herb Legg, a staunch public power man, stirred the pot by saying that right-to-vote candidates had recently won positions on the Thurston County PUD board because private power had "bought its votes."

The private-power Democrats from Spokane were not coming in with a right-to-vote plank, but they did have a plank, adopted by their county convention, that advocated "the competitive development of water resources of the Pacific Northwest." Sitting squarely on the fence, the Spokane County delegates said they favored "a fair distribution, designed to prevent the development of any monopoly, private, corporate, cooperative or public."

O'Brien made it clear he wanted to be permanent chairman of the convention. The Spokane County delegation came in determined to support a rival candidate, Senator Al Henry of White Salmon. O'Brien got the chairmanship, with Henry voting at the end to make it unanimous. That may have seemed like a reconciliation but, in fact, the Spokane County delegates were anything but reconciled to O'Brien's leadership. O'Brien's real troubles were just starting.

As permanent chairman, O'Brien had little to do with putting together the party platform, but he was later held responsible for it. The platform proved extremely controversial. It included a strong public power plank and a plank on individual rights that, in some conservatives' eyes, made the state Democratic party officially soft on communism.

The platform called for amendment of the McCarran Act, the federal law that required communists to register with the government, and the elimination of state loyalty oaths. The King County convention had voted to amend the McCarran Act. Members of the Spokane County delegation led the fight against the citizens' rights plank. When they lost, Representative Bill McCormick of Spokane said, "I will no longer support this platform." O'Brien tried to cut off McCormick, saying that there was nothing to discuss because "there is nothing before us now."

"Yes, there is," McCormick said. "The thing that is before us is the reason that I am leaving this convention. Anyone who wants to come with me is welcome."

"Well, you are playing true to form."

"I am not playing true to form. If you remember, I was one of your supporters in the last Speaker's race when the vote was 30 to 29."

"You are a good friend of mine and a good legislator," O'Brien said. "I hate to see you do this."

But McCormick did it. He led the Spokane delegation out of the convention. A handful of delegates from King County and elsewhere left, too.

"This platform is the Communist Manifesto," railed one of the Spokane delegates, Joseph Hurley. A former legislator who was married to Representative Margaret Hurley, he said, "I would be excommunicated from my church. I couldn't go to mass in the morning if I had to support the thing."

One of the King County labor leaders who opposed the platform, James Bender, said, "Labor supports the Supreme Court. [The Court] has upheld the McCarran Act.

We couldn't endorse anyone who goes contrary to this."

The walkout was not a total surprise. And it certainly was not spontaneous. Some people close to the Spokane delegation had speculated before the convention ever began that if the party adopted a public power plank, the Spokane delegates would leave. Now, Herb Legg charged that "the action of a few Spokane Democrats in leaving the Democratic convention was apparently planned in advance as a publicity stunt to gain approbation from those supporting their minority position . . . on a few issues."

The party's vice-chairman Florence Davis shot back: "As I personally convened with this delegation from 11:00 P.M. to 2:00 A.M. under the leadership of state Representative William McCormick, it is very grievous to think that any delegation which took its job this seriously would plan a cheap—and I said cheap—publicity stunt."

The walkout itself may have been a stunt, but the disaffection it dramatized was real. O'Brien, although he was not responsible for the Democratic platform, could not stand clear of it. A Spokane representative who walked out of the convention, William May, said, "When Spokane walked out the door, the Speakership [for O'Brien] walked out the window."

Representative William Day, a Spokane chiropractor known as "Big Daddy," announced he would run on Spokane County's own platform. He said, "Our big objection [to the state convention] was that apparently a group of hard-core ultraliberals has succeeded in getting control of the party. . . . We did not attempt to endorse private power as against public power, but we feel that the Spokane County Democratic platform on power was best for the interests of the people." After the November election, in which the Democrats won a narrow three-seat majority, the press reported that Day would probably run against O'Brien for Speaker.

The election campaigns had seen a lot of right-wing rhetoric and outright slander used against some candidates who had been strongly identified with public power in the filibuster of 1961. Anticommunism made a better rallying cry than did private power. One of the legislators who got dumped—in the primary—was John Goldmark, whom O'Brien had made chairman of Ways and Means. Goldmark was the young liberals' ideal, but he did not have a warm enough personality to win supporters among the bystanders. He wound up taking some of the heat for the filibuster.

Goldmark was accused of being under communist influence on the grounds that his wife, Sally, had been a member of the Communist party for a brief period years before. Goldmark later won a libel suit against his accusers, but that did not help him in the campaign. His advocacy of public power was not the overt issue, but it was at least a curious coincidence that, although he had already served several terms, only in the aftermath of the fight over House Bill 197 did anyone learn of—or become concerned about—his wife's communist affiliation in the 1930s.

There was no question where Goldmark, who lived within Washington Water Power's political sphere of influence, stood on public power. Indeed, the month before the primary, he wrote to O'Brien—in a letter that was published in the press—asking the Legislative Council to investigate the private power lobbying in Washington, D.C., that had prevented Congress from authorizing construction of a steam generating plant at the N-reactor at Hanford. (At issue was use of a government-owned nuclear reactor to generate power. The plant was subsequently built. It marked the first adventure in nuclear power for the Washington Public Power Supply System. Despite WPPSS's later misfortunes, the plant itself worked well.) "I request that the Legislative Council investigate a shocking betrayal of the interests of the people of the state," Goldmark wrote O'Brien. "It is a matter of common knowledge that the private power lobby killed the project."

O'Brien was sure ever afterward—as were Herb Legg and other people—that private power was really behind the 1962 attack on Goldmark. The president of a private utility later told Legg that private power had used some $20,000—a considerable sum at the time—to change the makeup of the legislature. It picked its races carefully, investing about $1,000 wherever it chose to get involved. (Nevertheless, utility executives channeled less money than they were given credit for into the campaigns.)

Legg believed that when Goldmark and some of the other young men in his circle were defeated, the Democratic party lost its "ginger," its main source of new ideas. And O'Brien lost support within the caucus. Legg perceived, though, that the defeat of Goldmark and other public power partisans was not the only strike against O'Brien as he approached the Speakership battle for 1963. Another was the noticeable "bitterness" between O'Brien and Si Holcomb, who intrigued against him.

The anticommunist rhetoric provided a new wrinkle, but the same old people were still trying to accomplish the same old things. By late November, some of the legislators who had supported Leonard Sawyer for Speaker two years before were reportedly supporting "Big Daddy" Day. After talking with people in eastern Washington, Bob

Perry announced, "You can safely say that O'Brien is not going to be Speaker."

You could not prove it by the vote at the Democratic caucus on December 12. The Democrats voted thirty-eight for O'Brien, nine for Day, and three for Dick Kink. It was the fifth straight time the caucus had chosen O'Brien. He had won before by margins much narrower than 38 to 9. But his victory was far from secure. Thirty-eight votes did not give him a majority in the House. Normally, Democrats who voted against him in caucus would have supported him routinely on the floor of the House. This time, some Democrats who had voted against O'Brien in caucus had no intention of voting for him later on. Day, Perry, Margaret Hurley, and Representative Chet King of Raymond said, in fact, that they would not vote for O'Brien in the House.

Right after the caucus, Dan Evans, the Republican floor leader, said he was delighted by the division in the Democratic ranks. Within a week, there were rumors of a coalition between the dissident Democrats and the Republicans.

The rumors were on target. Bob Perry, very much on the Washington Water Power payroll, was working from the Democratic side. Evans and Slade Gorton were working from the Republican. The Republicans were not averse to joining forces with the private power Democrats. A coalition would enable them to control the House for the first time since 1953. Since the 1963 legislature might redistrict the state, and a Democratic legislature would create as many safe Democratic districts as possible, this might be the Republicans' last chance to control the House for a decade. "The Republicans formed the coalition because of redistricting," O'Brien said. "They'd been out of power for eight years. It gave them a chance to get back into power."

O'Brien recalled meeting with Evans, Gorton, and Representative Don Eldridge before the session to talk about committee chairmanships. He said later that "I could have been Speaker if I'd given them just half of all the committee chairmanships, half of everything. Then they would have let me continue on as Speaker. But the caucus wouldn't agree to that, and if I'd done it, I would have had a very miserable time. I just couldn't take people out of key committee chairmanships that had been so loyal to me over a long period of time."

In contrast, Day said he was "absolutely" willing to give the Republicans some chairmanships.

A week before the session began, Perry said, "O'Brien is as dead as last year's garbage. He's through. He's finished. He's *not* going to get it."

Day and Perry could not resist talking, but the Republicans played everything very close to the vest. There were no real leaks of the fact that they were prepared to vote en masse for an insurgent Democrat. "It was probably the best-kept political secret of the time I've been in politics," Slade Gorton recalled years later, when he was Washington's senior U.S. Senator. There was nothing to leak because the leadership "never allowed the Republican caucus to take a vote on the issue until about thirty minutes before we were sworn in."

By that time, all the House Republicans were safely shut away behind closed doors in caucus, away from Democratic persuasion or arm-twisting. Democratic legislators filed in and out of O'Brien's office all morning. Half an hour before the session started, Day and Perry took their seats. "Something go wrong?" Perry was asked. "You're not smiling." The Republicans simply were not around.

O'Brien and his supporters had been pretty sure they could count on the votes of at least three Republicans, but they could never reach the Republicans to talk with them. "They had a difficult time forming the coalition," O'Brien said. "Because of my friendship with many of the Republican legislators. They locked people up in the caucus room upstairs until twelve o'clock, when they came out. Then they put the House under the call of the House. They did that to keep their people away from us. We felt we had members of their caucus who were going to vote with us."

It took the House three votes to deny O'Brien his fifth term as Speaker. Bob Schaefer of Vancouver, who had been one of O'Brien's floor leaders, started by nominating O'Brien. Then Margaret Hurley nominated Day. It was Hurley whose dramatic wheelchair appearance had given O'Brien the one vote he needed to become Speaker in 1955. But Hurley was one of the Spokane hard core, and she was evidently miffed at O'Brien because someone else's bill had been placed ahead of hers in the previous session. She had already stated publicly that she would not support O'Brien again for Speaker. Dan Evans was nominated by the Republicans.

The first roll-call vote went forty-five for O'Brien, six for Day, forty-eight for Evans. All the Republicans voted for Evans. The six Democrats who voted for Day included Hurley, Day himself, Bill McCormick, Bob Perry, Dick Kink, and Chet King. On the second roll call, one vote shifted from O'Brien to Day. Then, on the third, all but one of the Republicans swung their votes to Day. The final count was one for Evans, forty-one for O'Brien, fifty-seven for Day. O'Brien's reign as Speaker was over.

It was "the only time I ever saw John out-flummoxed," recalled James Dolliver, then a Republican political staffer, later an administrative assistant to Governor Dan Evans, and eventually a justice of the state supreme court. "He didn't realize what was happening until the knife was going in." When O'Brien saw what was going on, after the voting had started, "he came storming down the center aisle." But it was too late.

Slade Gorton said O'Brien's vain effort to make a deal with Evans while the voting was in progress was "the most dramatic thing I've ever seen."

O'Brien had set his heart on the Speakership twenty years before. He had won it. He had gloried in it. Now, he had just watched it slip away. When the vote was over, he stood up and condemned the maneuvering that had cost him the gavel. One listener wrote that his voice shook with emotion. "This was a very bad mistake," he said. "It was a low type of political maneuvering. It was dishonest and immoral. There should be a code of ethics—even among legislators."

As O'Brien "continued to rail at the Republicans and Democrats who'd thwarted him," Adele Ferguson wrote in the *Bremerton Sun,* "voices rose, and the man who once was king was obviously just another House member talking too long."

The coalition had been forged to defeat John O'Brien, but its forging had consequences that went beyond O'Brien's political downfall and sense of betrayal. Ultimately, it enabled Republicans to control the House throughout the turbulent transitional period of the late 1960s and early 1970s. It helped seat Republican Dan Evans in the governor's office during those same years.

In the short run, it made the 1963 legislative session unusually tense and acrimonious. "This legislature has been bought and paid for by private power," Mark Litchman said as the O'Brien forces filibustered to keep the coalition from organizing the House. "I am aware, of my personal knowledge, that private power entered this fight. They controlled Olympia, and they spent $35,000 for Mr. Perry and others to get elected two years ago," said Litchman, who Perry's seatmate. "I understand the amount is in excess of one hundred or two hundred thousand dollars now. Mr. Perry is an employee of private power and has been in their employ for two or three years. So don't kid me who is being bought and who is being sold. . . . The dissident members of my own party . . . for their own personal gain—even for a committee chairmanship—are displaying a form of buying and selling legislators."

A Republican legislator yelled "Throw him out!" but Perry said, "Let him speak." Afterward, Perry told the press that Litchman's statement was "ridiculous." He said, "I didn't get a cent." This was the same Bob Perry who would later testify under oath that he was actually on the payroll of a Washington Water Power subsidiary at the time. Asked to describe for a grand jury the services he performed for Washington Water Power at the legislature, he said, "They used the term 'inside man.'" Sixteen years later, an executive vice-president of Washington Water Power, William A. Lowry, said publicly that "No efforts were made to conceal the payments made by the corporation to Mr. Perry." Perry claimed that McCormick had been on Washington Water Power's payroll, too.

All this was, if not known, at least strongly suspected by a lot of people in Olympia at the time. Discussing the coalition at the Cascadian Hotel in Wenatchee, state Senator Jerry Hanna said, "There is no question in my mind that underriding all this is the public versus private power situation." Representative Horace Bozarth said, "The question is: are we going to let an all-powerful lobbyist party control the legislature?"

The coalition responded with a show of moral indignation. Evans challenged Mark Litchman to repeat his accusations off the floor of the House. "The only way he would make that statement is because he's under immunity of the House," Evans said.

The fact was that although the Republicans had purely political goals of their own, without the power issue, there would never have been a coalition. O'Brien would have been Speaker for a fifth term. Not that O'Brien's defeat had much immediate bearing on the fate of public power; the right-to-vote bill was not revived. Public power had been a big Democratic issue in the 1962 campaign, and Rosellini, who had pretty well kept hands off in 1961, had let it be known that he would probably veto any right-to-vote bill that passed. In addition, the takeover of private power property was no longer an imminent threat. Two years before, it had seemed likely that the Thurston County PUD would try to take property from Puget Power, but the 1962 election had packed the PUD board with people who were committed to doing no such thing.

The loyal Democrats were not defending public power when the session started; they were simply obstructing coalition efforts to get the session underway. They filibustered for days, preventing the House from establishing the names and sizes of committees, keeping it from getting organized and settling down to business, piling pointless amendment on amendment, and protesting the election of the coalition Speaker. The press reported that the filibuster was in part over committee chairmanships, and that the regular Democrats wanted above all else to get O'Brien a seat on the Rules Committee. O'Brien denied this. "McCormick offered his seat on the Rules Committee to me," he said, "but I wouldn't accept it."

O'Brien was bombarded with indignant editorials about the Democrats' delaying tactics and about what struck some observers as his personal vendetta against the coalition. If O'Brien did feel a sense of personal outrage that went beyond the normal sting of defeat, it was only natural. He had gained, held, and exercised power by understanding perfectly, in minute detail, how the system worked. He had respected the system and the hierarchy that it established. Under the system, as it had usually worked, he would now have been Speaker for a fifth term. But the leaders of the coalition had disregarded—had brazenly flouted—the system. And they had won.

(O'Brien wanted very much to be Speaker again, but there were limits beyond which he would not go. Late one night, he got a telephone call from a man who said that if he wanted to wreck the coalition, here was all the ammunition he needed: the new Speaker was going around with the man's wife, who worked at the capitol. O'Brien refused to use the allegations.)

The loyalist Democrats expelled the seven members of their party who had voted for Day on the second ballot from the House Democratic caucus. For the whole 1963 session, those expelled legislators were welcome in neither the Democratic nor the Republican caucus; when other legislators left the room to caucus, they had to sit in the House chamber and wait.

The coalition finally did organize the House. Republi-

can leader Slade Gorton moved to table all the Democrats'
delaying amendments, then to adjourn. The slate was then
clean, and the coalition could do as it pleased. When
O'Brien said he was outraged by the Republican maneuver, the *Daily Olympian* commented that outrage was a
strange reaction for the man who had proved himself "the
fastest gavel north of the Pecos."

Gorton later characterized O'Brien as "a tough and
rather bitter floor leader" in 1963. He undoubtedly was.
It was a bitter time. O'Brien himself remembered legislators arguing over the coalition in Olympia restaurants.
But it was not all bitterness. A few weeks into the session,
O'Brien broke the tension in the House by standing up
and wishing Day a happy birthday.

Nevertheless, Day did not have an easy time of it. He
did not have many people on his side. O'Brien said years
later that Day "took more of a battering on the rostrum
than anyone I've ever seen."

(Battered or not, Day managed to cause O'Brien a fair
measure of trouble. After the 1963 session ended, O'Brien
attended a meeting of the National Conference of State
Legislative Leaders in Boston. He found, on his return,
that Day would not let him be reimbursed for his expenses. He got in touch with his friend, Republican leader
Tom Copeland, who wrote to Day: "It is my understanding that John O'Brien attended [the conference] as a
member of the Executive Committee and that his expense
money was not allowed by your action. If you will recall,
during the session the question arose on the floor of the
House at which time I indicated that these funds would
be available to Mr. O'Brien for this purpose. This certainly was not done by me in a facetious manner, and at
that time, it was my understanding that it had your full

concurrence." A little later, Copeland sent O'Brien a note saying: "All is well—send your voucher to Si [Holcomb].")

The Republicans got eleven of twenty-one committee chairmanships. Some rather unexpected Democrats were offered the rest. When neophyte Representative Sam Smith, later a Seattle City Councilman, was named chairman of the Committee on Local Government, he reportedly burst out laughing. Smith refused the chairmanship. "They offered me everything I could want." he recalled, "but I just smiled and said 'No dice.'" When the coalition took over, Smith said, "I knew *what* was going on, but I didn't know *why*." He did not want to get tangled up in it, whatever it was. He never regretted his decision. Bitterness over the coalition "lasted for years," Smith said. "I don't think [the people who took leading roles] ever forgave each other."

The coalition and its consequences hastened, if they did not actually bring about, a major changing of the guard. Whether the guard would have changed anyway is a moot point. There is reason to suppose that something would have happened. An unusually able group of young Republican legislators, including Dan Evans, Slade Gorton and Joel Pritchard, later to become a congressman and lieutenant governor, had been sitting in the House for four to eight years without ever being in the majority. The coalition gave them their first opportunity to exercise power. It led, more or less directly, to a legislative redistricting the following session that gave them control of the House through the end of the decade. And it helped in no small measure to make Dan Evans governor.

The previous fall, Evans and O'Brien, as their parties' legislative leaders, had appeared in a number of debates. Both were plausible candidates for governor. When

O'Brien lost the Speakership, talk about his becoming governor stopped abruptly.

The coalition did not make Evans Speaker in O'Brien's place. But it did give Evans and his colleagues a platform for attacking Rosellini. And it enhanced Evans's stature, not so much with the electorate as within the Republican party. Evans had not made his mark in the House as a natural leader. One old friend remembers him as shy about speaking, the kind of person who literally hid behind pillars. O'Brien once recalled that, when he was Speaker and Evans was Republican floor leader, "occasionally, when I wanted to do something administratively, I would bypass Dan Evans. We used to characterize him as someone with a slide rule. He was an engineer, and he wouldn't do anything unless—it had to be right down to the minute degree. And sometimes he was very stubborn. I had a good relationship with some legislators on the other side, and we would bypass Dan."

Evans was not getting bypassed any more. The fact that he held the coalition together on almost every significant vote during the long 1963 session made other Republican legislators think of him as a man who got things done.

Not that Evans's election was a sure thing in 1964. Even after he won the Republican nomination, the favorite had to be Albert Rosellini, who was seeking a third term. But Evans ran a very energetic campaign. His was the first campaign in the state to do a lot of serious doorbelling. He got help from state conservatives who deserted the Goldwater presidential campaign after it was taken over by what they considered the lunatic fringe. And Evans turned out to be great on TV. So, despite the fact that Democrat Lyndon Johnson won the presidential election by a landslide, and the Democrats won Congress and both houses of the state legislature, Evans was elected the Republican governor of Washington.

Evans turned out to be very much a man for the times. Times had changed. Styles were shifting. That was the year the Beatles landed in America. In Olympia, the old, formal social life was fading fast. The Tyee Motel, opened in Tumwater at the end of the 1950s, was becoming the new social center. The Tyee and the Olympian were worlds apart. The new motel was an oasis of midcentury kitsch. It had swimming pools and loud music and plenty of vinyl. The politicans and lobbyists flocked to it. At one point, it had the busiest bar in the state. Lobbying techniques changed to accommodate the new environment. When people dined at the Olympian, meals were formal, and a lobbyist usually either took someone to dinner or kept his distance. In the Tyee, with its informality, a lobbyist could just sit down uninvited at someone's table for a quick chat. The stately world of the Olympian, which O'Brien had made his political milieu, was fast becoming the world of the past.

Substance soon seemed nearly as different as style. John F. Kennedy was assassinated in November 1963, but his presidency had transformed the tone of national politics. The civil rights movement had made racial equality a national concern. The March on Washington, highlighted by Martin Luther King's great "I Have a Dream" speech, took place in 1963. The "free speech movement" tied up the Berkeley campus. The Vietnam War was in the news more and more. Kennedy had launched the Apollo Space Program. The nation's economy was booming. Evans fit right in with the new issues and the new style. Whether he was an effective governor is another question. He was, even in the eyes of many Democrats, the right man for the middle and late 1960s.

Even if there had been no coalition, could O'Brien have filled that role? He was closely identified with the politics of the 1950s. He did not have Evans's youth or his image of high morality, of being almost above politics. It may be that, given the tidal change in politics at that time, if the coalition had not derailed him, something else would have.

He might not even have run. He did not run for lieutenant governor. He did not run for mayor. After the coalition took power, O'Brien was discussed as a candidate for Congress from the 7th District. Reportedly, he had been toying with the idea. But he did not relish the thought of moving his family across the country and he did not want to be too far from his businesses. Julia Butler Hansen, by then serving her second term in Congress, thought he should take the plunge. "I tried to persuade John to run for that [7th District] seat," Hansen said years later, but "he wouldn't run at all."

"It just wasn't my cup of tea," O'Brien explained.

"I just figured after that," Hansen said, "that John was a perpetual Speaker candidate."

O'Brien's heart stayed on the rostrum. And he would wield the gavel many times in years to come. But the old power would never return.

VII

Becoming an Elder Statesman

O'BRIEN'S ROAD BACK TO THE ROSTRUM PROVED LONG and circuitous. The same coalition that had denied him the Speakership was revived long enough in 1965 to take the Democrats out of power until 1973. O'Brien did not get to preside over the breakup of the Democratic empire, as it were, but he was in on the finish. The Democrats won the House again in 1964. For the first time in twenty years, O'Brien was not a candidate for Speaker. After the bitterness of 1963, he was no longer sure he had the stomach for a Speakership fight. He got off to a slow start. By the time he seriously considered a run, another Democrat, Bob Schaefer, had already lined up some of the votes on which O'Brien would normally have counted. He decided not to try it. But he was surprised by some of the people who urged him to run. "Bill McCormick, the leader of the coalition, wanted me to run for Speaker next time," O'Brien recalled. "They all wanted me to run for Speaker. The group that took us out wanted me to run against Bob Schaefer. Bill McCormick called me at three in the morning at the hotel where we were meeting and urged me to be a candidate." O'Brien did not run, and Schaefer was elected. O'Brien was elected majority floor leader.

Rosellini was still governor when the legislature opened, but he would leave office in a few days. O'Brien and the other Democrats wanted to pass a redistricting bill before Evans came in. They tried, but they could not do it. Boeing and other large interests lobbied heavily against them. The Republicans, the coalition Democrats, and a few others stood fast. On Rosellini's last day in office, O'Brien, Leonard Sawyer, and Gary Grant, who was the House Democrats' main man for redistricting, tried to increase their number of sure votes from forty-eight to fifty. They failed. They could not even bring a redistricting bill to the floor. From then on, any redistricting plan that the legislature passed would have to be acceptable to a Republican governor.

The time-honored solution to redistricting problems—just forgetting the whole thing—was no longer an option. Redistricting had been the big task facing the 1963 legislature, but, despite having met for a special session of record length, the legislators had not managed to do the job. Now, they had no choice. In May 1963, a three-judge federal panel ruled that the Washington redistricting law passed in 1957 to undo the initiative of 1956 was "invidiously discriminatory" in its underrepresentation of urban areas. It was, therefore, unconstitutional. The next year, the United States Supreme Court issued the "one-man-one-vote" ruling that required representation in proportion to population, killing any slight hope the state might have had of a successful appeal. The Supreme Court also agreed that the Washington law was unconstitutional. A federal court subsequently ordered the legislature to pass a redistricting law before doing anything else.

It was not easy. A court order did not negate the political process. Some legislators said they would not vote for a redistricting bill unless they got certain key committee assignments. Evans, for his part, said he would veto any bill that failed to treat the Republicans "fairly."

Evans did veto a couple of redistricting bills. The debate dragged on for forty-seven days. It ended, finally, with a bill that O'Brien and most other House Democrats disliked. They might have averted it, but O'Brien had, by his own reckoning, miscalculated badly. He, Schaefer, and other legislative leaders met in Evans's office to work out an agreement. O'Brien and the other House Democrats "came to the conclusion that we couldn't get anywhere, so we walked out of the governor's office." They assumed the others would not dare reach an agreement without them. "That, I think, was a big mistake because when we walked out, they started working on [district boundary] lines themselves. Governor Evans and Bob Greive and Slade Gorton and others drew the lines. Bob Greive once said, 'When you left the room, there wasn't any opposition.'"

Greive himself said later that "there was nothing we could do. He just left us flat. It was either [work out a compromise then and there] or they were going to go to a master [that is, a neutral expert who would redraw the lines without regard for political considerations]." Greive figured O'Brien had to worry about keeping his own caucus together as well as redistricting. "There were some hotheads," he said. "John had to think of the short *and* long term. You only hold a position of leadership as long as somebody is willing to follow." O'Brien said he really did think nothing was being accomplished at the meeting, but he conceded that "some members of our caucus sort of felt we shouldn't be a part of it" at all.

Once the lines were drawn and a bill was brought to the floor, O'Brien said, "the same group that formed the coalition voted with the Republicans on redistricting." Some previously loyal Democrats joined, too. "I remember [former Democratic floor leader Mark] Litchman went and gave them the fiftieth vote. [Litchman] was in Seattle, and we had to hold up the whole House for three or four hours until he could get down there, and then he votes against us. He gets up on the floor of the House and says, 'I'm probably going to get shafted for doing this,' and I got the microphone and I said, 'You're going to get shafted right now!' He started talking about his conscience, and when people start talking about their conscience I always hold my breath, because invariably, they're going to vote against you."

The old coalition prevailed. "It was just one of those things," O'Brien said. "It was very bitter to lose that bill."

(O'Brien and Litchman did not always wind up on opposite sides of the fence. In the next session, they both sponsored a moderate gun control bill. That did not go over well in all quarters. One morning at eight o'clock, a gun-toting man wearing a hat covered with marksmanship medals walked into O'Brien's office and announced he was going to shoot both O'Brien and Litchman. O'Brien was not yet in. His secretary gave the man a cup of coffee and told him she was a member of the National Rifle Association. They talked about the NRA until O'Brien arrived. By that time, the man had calmed down enough to shake O'Brien's hand and chat with him.)

The election of 1966 gave the Republicans control of the House for the first time since 1953. Redistricting had done the trick. O'Brien, running in the 35th District instead of the 33rd, got reelected without difficulty, but other

Democrats were less fortunate. The legislature elected in 1966 contained a lot of new faces. Urban areas were better represented, and the new, urban-oriented legislators were more inclined to spend money for state services. Evans had seized control of a progressive agenda. He was advocating tax reform, rapid transit, and pollution control.

Those high-minded goals did not keep the actual day-to-day business of the House from being bitterly partisan. The Democrats nominated O'Brien for Speaker as a matter of form. The majority Republicans elected Don Eldridge, who was not reluctant to cut Democratic orators off. The Democrats were frustrated.

But they were not left totally out in the cold. The Evans Republicans did not control the right wing of their own party, so they could not pass legislation without Democratic support. O'Brien, as the Democratic leader, was in a position to make deals and to act as the spoiler.

A lot of Evans's progressive legislation did not pass. He wanted a flat-rate income tax, but the Democrats killed it. Evans's tax proposal brought up the old ideological conflict between a flat-rate and a graduated tax. O'Brien, still convinced that a graduated tax was the only fair way to go, joined organized labor and the League of Women Voters in opposing the flat-rate tax.

Indirectly—and inadvertently—he kept the Republicans from passing it. Just as the issue was coming to a head, he went to New York for a weekend meeting of the National Conference of State Legislative Leaders. Eldridge had promised him that the tax bill would not be moved until he returned. But in O'Brien's absence, things started going the Republicans' way. They seemed to have the two-thirds majority they needed to amend the Constitution, so they tried to move the bill despite Eldridge's promise. They could not do it; some Democrats who favored the bill refused to vote until O'Brien got back. The Republicans had to wait until Monday. When the legislators went home for the weekend, some Democrats who had been willing to vote for Evans's tax proposal got an earful from irate constituents. By the time they returned to Olympia, the two-thirds majority had melted away.

(Despite Democratic rhetoric, the choice was not really between a flat-rate tax and a graduated tax. It was between a flat-rate tax and a higher sales tax. The legislature wound up raising the sales tax from 4.2 to 4.5 percent and increasing the gas tax from 7.5 to 9 cents per gallon, making both taxes the highest in the continental United States.)

A utility right-to-vote bill finally slipped through the House, and narrowly missed being approved by the Senate. Actually, the friction between public and private power had decreased. Facing what both foresaw as a period of huge increases in the demand for power, both were determined to build new generating plants, and they might need each other in order to do it. The landmark power legislation of 1967 was a law that enabled private and public utilities to own generating facilities together.

But some legislators were still fighting the old battles, so a right-to-vote amendment was tacked onto the joint ownership law in the House. It caught opponents napping and sailed through on a vote of 59 to 38. The amendment "came sneaking up on us like a thief in the night," O'Brien said. He complained that "this bill serves no useful purpose. There's ample protection for private power now. This bill is going to cause a lot of hard feelings, because it is being pushed through in bad faith."

"Big Daddy" Day, a cosponsor of the amendment, replied, "I regret that Mr. O'Brien calls this bad faith. . . . When we were thwarted by over one hundred roll call votes on amendments in 1961 is a better example of bad faith."

They were thwarted again in 1967. Evans said he would veto the legislation, and it failed in a senate committee by one vote.

(For O'Brien, the high point of the year would come long after he left Olympia. Meeting in San Francisco's elegant St. Francis Hotel—where Governor Ronald Reagan delivered the keynote address—the National Conference of State Legislative Leaders would elect him president for the coming year.)

Nineteen sixty-eight was a troubled year. Martin Luther King and Robert F. Kennedy were both assassinated, and in Seattle, as elsewhere, racial tension reached an all-time high. In September, O'Brien's Rainier community was up in arms over an "invasion" of Rainier Beach High School by armed Black Panthers. The home of state legislator David Sprague, who lived not far from O'Brien, was fire-bombed. Sprague, a white liberal, decided to drop out of politics. O'Brien helped persuade the Rainier Businessmen's Club to launch what the *Beacon Hill News* called "an all-out effort to help combat crime and violence." The club appointed a committee to meet with the mayor, the chief of police, and the city council to ask for more police protection for schools, businesses, and residential neighborhoods. O'Brien said that holdups and firebombings had already forced some firms out of business.

By the late 1960s, legislators were spending a lot of time thinking about racial issues. Some felt that O'Brien was a bit out of touch with the new concerns. He had grown up

with the politics of ethnic groups, but he was not conspicuous in debates over the rights of racial minorities.
One lobbyist who met O'Brien at that time "always considered him as kind of 'emeritus.'"

Still, O'Brien was not totally out of touch with minority
groups. In the late winter of 1969, eight Black Panthers
in leather jackets and berets showed up on the capitol steps
with rifles and shotguns, which they held at "salute arms"
for half an hour, watched by dozens of armed state troopers. The troopers had turned out en masse the day before
to meet the threat of a rumored Panther "invasion." The
fear of invasion from the ghettoes was very much a late-
sixties phenomenon, but it did not indicate that the times
had left John O'Brien entirely behind. To the contrary.
While the young men in berets brandished their weapons
on the capitol steps, and while Seattle Panther leader Aaron
Dixon read a list of demands to the Senate Ways and Means
Committee, Dixon's younger brother Michael, in coat and
tie, was inside the capitol working as a page for John
O'Brien.

O'Brien was still tuned into the needs and desires of
the cities. Whenever the city of Seattle wanted something
in Olympia, its officials and lobbyists went to see him. One
city lobbyist found the experience of going back to
O'Brien's big office almost ceremonial—but he also found
that, unlike some other legislative leaders, O'Brien never
expected to be treated like royalty. (In fact, O'Brien's young
children occasionally played in his big office on the third
floor of the capitol. Once, state patrol officers looked up
and saw the lively O'Brien kids playing on the narrow ledge
outside the third-floor windows. The cops rushed upstairs, but the kids saw them coming and scattered before
they arrived.)

O'Brien's pet bills in 1969 included one that let parochial and other private school students attend public schools for courses not offered at their own schools, and another that would have established a Puget Sound port authority. The first bill passed, and it has had lasting effects. The second was doomed from the start. O'Brien had concluded that competition among Puget Sound ports was wasteful. The logic was irrefutable, but the politics were hopeless; small ports feared domination by Seattle. The bill did not pass. Nevertheless, O'Brien would keep reviving it over the years—sometimes, his friends at the Port of Seattle just wanted to send a message to smaller ports— and the idea of a regional port authority became firmly identified with John O'Brien.

Most of Dan Evans's big ideas fared no better than the idea of a regional port. The legislature could not agree on a tax reform proposal during the regular session, and in May, far into a special session, Evans got Democratic and Republican leaders together in his office to work out a compromise. When O'Brien and senate majority leader Bob Greive kept the group from reaching agreement, Evans enlarged the group so that they would be outvoted. Evans said later that O'Brien and Greive had been "outgunned." The group did work out a compromise. It decided to put a flat-rate income tax of 3.5 percent before the people, reduce the sales tax, and, if the flat-rate tax passed, let the people vote on a graduated-rate income tax—which O'Brien and the Democrats still advocated— in 1975. O'Brien spoke in favor of the compromise, and the legislature passed it, but the voters rejected the flat-rate tax, so a graduated tax never even got onto the ballot.

The futile battles over a state income tax went on. The

futile battles over public power finally ended. There were no longer any imminent threats of private utilities being taken over by PUDs. Both private and public utilities were obsessed with the building of new nuclear plants. Besides, Ken Billington realized he could no longer avoid defeat in the legislature; he got together with the chief executives of Washington Water Power, Puget Power, and Pacific Power and Light and worked out a truce. The issue that had made O'Brien a hero eight years before, and that had cost him the Speakership six years before, had, for all practical purposes, ceased to exist.

The Democrats did not win the House in 1970, but it looked before the election as if they might, so ambitious Democratic legislators campaigned for leadership positions. O'Brien was one of at least four men trying seriously to line up votes for the Speakership. Another was Leonard Sawyer. Sawyer had by then learned to manipulate the patronage system that the Committee on Committees, introduced when O'Brien first won the Speakership, had made possible. As Frank Brouillet saw it, "John was up there running the ship while someone else was down there messing with the engine."

Someone else had, in fact, taken control of the engine. The Democrats did not win, but Sawyer did. He clearly had a majority of the caucus behind him for minority leader, so O'Brien gracefully withdrew from the contest. Sawyer was nominated by acclamation. This was not a behind-the-scenes triumph of private utilities, nor was it muscle-flexing by young turks. It was simply affirmation of a shift in the balance of power.

On the Republican side, Don Eldridge did not run again, and O'Brien's friend, Tom Copeland, who had served as interim Speaker between legislative sessions, was dumped in favor of Tom Swayze. Copeland lost partly because some Republicans thought he had been too friendly with the Democrats, most conspicuously with John O'Brien.

Copeland had wanted very much to be Speaker. Banking on his desire, Republican Representative Paul Barden put together a coalition of fifteen renegade Republicans and forty Democrats who were willing to back him. O'Brien was prepared to join the coalition—he talked it over with Copeland and made his position clear—but Copeland backed out.

In time-honored fashion, the 1971 legislature failed to pass a redistricting bill, and a special session at the start of 1972 failed, too. A court then appointed University of Washington geographer Richard Morrill to do the job. Democratic legislators were appalled by the results, but they need not have been; the election of 1972—in which voters approved a Campaign Disclosure Law and a Shorelines Management Act, and elected Dan Evans to a third term as governor—gave them control of both the senate and the House.

O'Brien's old rivals, Leonard Sawyer and August Mardesich, became Speaker and senate majority leader. Both were able men. Neither had led the majority before. They were logical choices. And yet, although the world had changed drastically, the Democrats' idea of new blood was men who had been waiting in the wings for a dozen years.

Sawyer was a master politician, but he was not a particularly good presiding officer. He did not choose to spend much time on the rostrum running the House. That task fell to John O'Brien. When Sawyer was elected Speaker of the House, O'Brien was elected to his first term as

Speaker pro tem. That put him in a position to preside—which he had always loved doing—whenever Sawyer did not. And Sawyer did not most of the time.

The House needed a strong hand on the rostrum. A change of legislative power is always accompanied by partisan jousting, and this time the majority was changing after eight years. The Republicans were often on their feet shouting in protest. O'Brien kept them in their places with a quick gavel and frequent recesses to caucus. Helen Sommers, watching as a first-term Democratic representative, saw that "he was very astute in citing past precedents and finding the rulings he wanted." Still, "I remember one time he was cornered, and he just said, 'Oh, that's moot.' Everyone had to laugh." Jim Dwyer, who served as caucus attorney for the House Democrats, recalled, "He'd announce the result before the buttons were pushed."

There was not much tension within the House Democratic caucus. But over in the senate, where Mardesich had unseated long-time Democratic leader Bob Greive, the atmosphere was very tense, not least because Mardesich seemed vengeful. Dwyer recalled years later that "people were afraid to buy Greive a drink . . . Greive would walk into a bar and people would move away." The House was different. Sawyer had no lingering rivals for the Speakership. His ally Bob Perry, considered one of the most powerful men in Olympia, was chairman of the Transportation and Utilities Committee. He was still working on behalf of Washington Water Power.

Perry had begun planning with Washington Water Power vice-president and lobbyist Jerry Buckley in 1972 to get around the Campaign Disclosure Law, which took effect at the beginning of 1973. The scheming of Perry and Buckley, which ultimately involved laundering tens of thousands of dollars through Hong Kong for payment to legislators, was not public knowledge when the legislature convened in 1973.

Nevertheless, it was to be a big year for corruption in national government. That spring, the Watergate scandal broke. Later in the year, Vice-President Spiro Agnew pled guilty to income tax evasion and resigned. With the executive branch of government falling into disrepute, legislatures all over the country became more assertive. Washington's legislature became as assertive as any. It not only had the desire but it finally had the tools to compete on even terms with the executive branch. Starting in 1973, the legislature acquired its own staff. If someone from the governor's office walked into a committee hearing, he no longer knew more about the subject at hand than anyone else in the room.

The development of a legislative staff and of legislative independence was primarily the work of Sawyer and Mardesich. The change was made abruptly in 1973. The Legislative Council disappeared at the end of June 1973 because its functions had largely been taken over by the legislature's new permanent research staff. The council in its heyday had seemed a political extension of John O'Brien; it did not amount to much before his Speakership, and it did not amount to much afterward. The new system had a life of its own; it represented a real institutional change.

A permanent staff was not the only novelty. Committees and subcommittees were to meet periodically even when the legislature was not in session. Their meetings were opened to the public. Historically, committee meetings had been closed and had been held at the chairman's whim. O'Brien and others who had lived with both systems soon found the new one a mixed blessing. In the old days, some members took favors from lobbyists, but at least the lobbyists did not see them cast their committee votes. Now, the lobbyists sat right in the front row. O'Brien realized that open committee meetings increased public scrutiny and public confidence, but he felt that they also increased the lobbyists' influence.

He did not realize that the relatively calm surface of governmental reform concealed the first stirrings of revolt—a revolt that would return him, however briefly, to the rostrum. Despite the staff and the open meetings, most junior legislators did not know what was going on. A small group of leaders called the shots in the House. Younger members could talk all they pleased in caucus, but then they would be largely ignored. Some grew frustrated; they arrived in Olympia hoping to change the world, but they were simply told how to vote, or else. Toward the end of the session, some started holding meetings about dumping Leonard Sawyer.

Ironically—or, maybe, appropriately— a private power issue in the next session helped precipitate the revolt against Sawyer that restored O'Brien temporarily to the Speakership. At the start of the next session, O'Brien was reelected unanimously as Speaker pro tem. In nominating him, Dave Ceccarelli talked about the classes in parliamentary procedure that O'Brien conducted for new members and called him "a parliamentary whiz."

There was no resumption of the fight between private utilities and PUDs. Public and private utilities were no longer fighting about takeovers. They were fighting to get money for nuclear construction. Both had bills in that session, and they agreed to leave each other's legislation alone.

The private utilities wanted a law that would permit them to charge customers for construction work in progress. Bob Perry, again chairman of the Transportation and Utilities Committee and still Washington Water Power's inside man, pushed the bill hard. Four years later, he said he knew of about $30,000 that had been spent to pass the bill, adding, "I'm sure there's a lot more."

When House Bill 435, reached the floor, many of the younger, more discontented Democrats tried to get it amended or reconsidered, but they failed. Sawyer voted with the bill's supporters, time after time. O'Brien voted with the opposition. He had been fighting private power too long to stop now. At a social function shortly afterward, he ran into Washington Water Power's Jerry Buckley, who said, "You never learn, do you? You never learn." Even years later, O'Brien described the incident with a trace of disgust. Perry and Sawyer twisted a lot of arms to pass the private power bill. They won the battle but they lost the war: Dan Evans vetoed it.

They wound up losing another war, too. The strong-armed passage of House Bill 435 helped touch off the legislative revolt that drove Sawyer from office and permanently changed the way the House did business.

The revolt was started by second-term Representative Rick Bender and freshman John McKibben. They built a list of allies very circumspectly. Only if a representative signed up himself was he allowed to see the other names on the list. Both McKibben and Bender were frustrated by their inability to influence the Democratic caucus. "We were convinced that the direction the caucus was taking was tied to a particular special interest," Bender said later. "We just had no voice in the caucus. Decisions in caucus were being made by a small group of people. We felt there was a certain lobbyist who had an easier time getting to the Speaker's office than some of the members."

"We came there to change the world in twenty-four or forty-eight hours," remembered Jim Boldt, who joined the dissidents early on, but "the leadership gave us few responsibilities except to vote yes."

O'Brien may have helped lay the groundwork for the revolt. Traditionally, first- and second-term legislators had been seen and not heard. They tended not to speak from the floor. In 1971, though, O'Brien started his classes in parliamentary procedure for freshman legislators. After that, new members knew the parliamentary forms. All of a sudden, people new to Olympia were standing up on the floor of the House and being heard, whetting their appetites for being taken seriously.

The private power bill "was my first encounter against the leadership," Bender recalled. It was "a good lesson. There were certain members who were told to support that bill . . . told that if they didn't support the Speaker on that issue, they wouldn't get any [of their own] legislation passed. [House Bill 435] was one of the bills that brought many of us together."

When House Bill 435 was on the floor, Jim Boldt moved to reconsider it. Perry stood up to rebut him. Then Boldt got a message to go up to the Speaker's rostrum. When he got there, "Len Sawyer asked if [he'd] really like to know who ran the place."

It was ironic. Before the 1961 session, when Sawyer had tried and narrowly failed to defeat O'Brien for the Speakership—again, doing private power's work—he had explained: "We simply feel that O'Brien has gotten too powerful and autocratic." Now, Sawyer himself was about to

walk the plank partly because people felt *he* was an au-
tocrat. Irony of ironies. John O'Brien—no longer in a position to wield the power he had wielded in the 1950s, but
still eager to have the gavel in his hand—would be there
to pick up the pieces.

The dissidents assumed they were not the only ones who
felt uneasy with the status quo. Rick Bender thought that
O'Brien himself "was unhappy. . . . He was really being
left out, too. I think he probably felt the same frustrations
we did." Bender had lunch with O'Brien at the Washington Athletic Club to fill him in on the revolt. O'Brien got
the impression that the dissidents objected mostly to Sawyer's less-than-simon-pure image. "I think," O'Brien said
later, that "they were concerned about Leonard Sawyer
because of some of his fund-raising activities, some of his
personal-service contracts."

That was at least part of the story. It was already known
that Sawyer had appeared before the grand jury investigating the West Seattle Bridge scandal, in which the city
engineer, Robert Gulino, who had been recommended for
the job by Bob Perry, had passed over the Seattle Design
Commission's four top candidates to give the engineering
contract to another firm. It was also known that Sawyer
had done work for the firm involved, and that his work
had included business trips to Papua, New Guinea, which
he had not reported on public disclosure forms. There
were rumors—totally unfounded—that he was about to
be indicted for his part in some scandal or other. The
same Democrats who disliked Sawyer's leadership style
disliked being represented by someone who carried with
him an aura of underhandedness.

O'Brien underestimated the depth of the discontent. "I
wasn't involved with either faction," he recalled. "I was

informed about what was happening, but I didn't know how serious it was." O'Brien told Bender that because of his position in the House, he could not join the dissident group, but he would keep the secret. He kept it well.

So did the rest of the group, up until the final hours. When a special legislative session began at the start of 1976, the dissidents met past midnight on each of the first three nights. They needed thirty-two votes in caucus to have a majority against Sawyer. O'Brien never did put his name on the list. As soon as they got the thirty-second vote, they moved.

On January 15, the dissidents went into a Democratic caucus meeting and gave Sawyer a petition asking him to resign. The next day, they told the press that Sawyer's "response was unacceptable." Sawyer hung on. On the tenth day of the session, the dissidents made a move on the floor of the House. One of them, Helen Sommers, recalled later that dumping Sawyer was "one of the most intense things I've ever been through." At the time, she wrote in a personal journal that "just before the session began, one of the overhead high-powered television lights exploded and showered glass down on the House chamber. We were already tense, and this small incident seemed to portend a day of exploding emotions. . . . I remember thinking, 'Ye gods, Leonard's world is crumbling around him, and he seems so unaware and so insensitive to the meaning of it all." Red-coated pages delivered to every member's desk a resolution that proclaimed: "The office of the Speaker of the House of Representatives is now declared vacant." The next day, with O'Brien presiding, Leonard Sawyer walked to the rostrum and resigned.

The dissidents had not made plans for taking power after Sawyer was out. They had not even lined up enough votes to elect one of their own members Speaker. They certainly did not want to throw up their hands and accept a Speaker from Sawyer's camp. So they turned to John O'Brien. O'Brien was already Speaker pro tem. He clearly knew how to run the House. Most important of all, he was someone they trusted. He was "a dependable quantity," John McKibben said later. "We knew we could count on him to be fair."

O'Brien was back where he wanted to be, not merely as Speaker pro tem but as interim Speaker. "I was presiding the day Leonard came out on the rostrum and took the microphone away from me and said he was resigning as Speaker," O'Brien recalled. "All we did was carry on."

In the political turmoil that followed Sawyer's downfall, Republicans were quick to challenge his rulings. "O'Brien won't acknowledge that these darts from the GOP opposition are sometimes merely obstreperous and shrill," Shelby Scates wrote in February. "But he says he has never before seen so many challenges—and he nearly broke his gavel last week" silencing a Republican speaker. "The new wave is learning what the old pros have always known," Scates wrote; "O'Brien is a 'Speaker's Speaker' when it comes to parliamentary rulings from the chair."

The Republicans were not his only problem. Some people claimed that the erstwhile dissidents were trying to be every bit as authoritarian as Sawyer, and they were trying to get O'Brien to run the House on their behalf. After he became interim Speaker, said O'Brien, "the faction that unseated Leonard served some ultimatums on me. They said that if I didn't do certain things they were going to take me out. But I never took them very seriously. . . . Whenever somebody doesn't like what I'm doing, I just weigh the comments. We had quite an interesting time.

They wanted Vito Ciecchi, who was Leonard's administrative assistant, to be immediately discharged. There was just some grumbling. It wasn't too strong, but they felt Vito shouldn't be part of the staff. Eventually, Vito did resign. Then they wanted me to change the Rules Committee. And I didn't. I didn't do anything, as a matter of fact, other than carry on." At the end of the session, Adele Ferguson wrote that O'Brien had given the anti-Sawyer Democrats a lot of leeway, but "he never let them go too far . . . or anyone else, either."

The election of 1976, held in the nation's post-Watergate malaise, turned up two political wild cards. Jimmy Carter became president of the United States. Dixy Lee Ray, a feisty, eccentric former zöology teacher, became the nominally Democratic governor of Washington. The Democrats won the House, so the anti-Sawyer dissidents were pitted against the old guard in the election for Speaker. O'Brien was not a candidate himself, but he wound up playing a crucial role. The dissidents nominated Al Baucr of Vancouver. The old guard was backing Sawyer's heir apparent, John Bagnariol. The caucus deadlocked. Thirty-two votes was the number needed to win. On the first vote, the count was Bauer thirty-one, Bagnariol thirty, with one abstention. It took seven ballots for Bagnariol to get the last two votes.

O'Brien provided one of them. He had reservations about John Bagnariol. As a member of the executive Rules Committee, he had seen Bagnariol's requests for personal service contracts, and he had a bad feeling about the way Sawyer's old chairman of Ways and Means tried to do business. But he could not very well vote for Bauer. One of Bauer's main supporters, Donn Charnley, wanted the position of Speaker pro tem. O'Brien wanted very much to keep the job. A vote for Bauer would have been a vote against himself. On the early rounds of voting, O'Brien passed. Finally, he voted for Bagnariol. Inadvertently, he had helped set the stage for another dramatic change of leadership.

But that still lay several years in the future. For the time being, Bagnariol was Speaker. What had the great revolt accomplished? It had not broken the logical line of succession within the Sawyer group. But it had changed the way the House operated. Things were run more democratically under Bagnariol than they had been under Sawyer, and they were to be run a lot more democratically under Bagnariol's successors. One thing that changed fundamentally was the method of choosing committee chairmen. Until the revolt, picking chairmen was basically the prerogative of the Speaker. After it, chairmanships had to be confirmed by a secret vote of the caucus. The system that O'Brien had found in 1941 and had used so masterfully in the 1950s and early 1960s was eroding, perhaps irreversibly. Within a decade, power was to be so dispersed that many legislators complained it was hard to get anything done.

A reformist lightning bolt had not struck randomly in the middle of Washington State. Similar kinds of political change were in the air all over the United States. This was, after all, still the era of Watergate. The United States Congress had relaxed its rigid seniority system in 1974. Other state legislatures were changing, too. The Washington legislature might have changed before the decade was out even if the revolt had never happened. Inevitable or not, O'Brien did not find the changes dramatic. There was no reason why he should. Old politics or new, he was secure in his post as Speaker pro tem.

The Ray governorship was marked by growing tension between the governor and the legislature, and between the governor and the press. O'Brien became one of Governor Ray's few defenders. Ironically, since he respected legislative tradition so much and had not always given Evans or his predecessors easy times, he now gained the reputation of being a legislator who always stood up for the governor. He respected Ray's intelligence and thought her policies were not all bad. He also figured that by feuding publicly with a governor of their own party, Democratic legislators were shooting themselves in the foot. Ray, for her part, evidently appreciated O'Brien's courtesy, his adherence to the forms. O'Brien thought, though, that it was unfortunate Governor Ray did not know more about politics. And he thought it was unfortunate that she did not know more about handling the press. Once, he and Ross Cunningham went to talk with her about getting along better with the media. She said, "John I'm too old to change now."

The election of 1978 produced another deadlock for the Speakership, this time between Democrats and Republicans. Each side had forty-nine votes. Clearly, neither would be able to elect a Speaker unless someone switched sides. O'Brien later recalled being told by a Republican leader that if he would only agree to a few procedural moves, he could be Speaker again. He wanted the Speakership, but not enough to take responsibility for forming a new coalition. The Democratic and Republican leaders met repeatedly to figure out how to organize the House. Finally, they decided to split the job, making John Bagnariol and Republican Duane Berentson co-Speakers.

Relations between the governor and the legislature did

not improve. O'Brien looked increasingly isolated as Ray's defender. He defended her partly "because everyone else was against her."

Both Bagnariol and Berentson were assumed to have gubernatorial ambitions, and those ambitions seemed responsible for some of the legislature's continuing efforts to stymie and embarrass Dixy Lee Ray. They were not the only legislative leaders who had their eyes on higher office. Senator Gordon Walgren, successor to August Mardesich as senate majority leader, wanted to be attorney general.

Bagnariol had rented the Swedish Club to kick off his official campaign on April 1. But there was to be no campaign for either Bagnariol or Gordon Walgren. On April 1, the two men were seen as plausible, if not inspiring, candidates for statewide office. On April 2, they were principals in "Gamscam," possibly the biggest political scandal in Washington history. The public learned that Bagnariol, Walgren, and lobbyist Patrick Gallagher, with whom Bagnariol had shared a house in Olympia and a checking account, had been the targets of an FBI sting. The legislators and lobbyist were subsequently charged with racketeering, conspiracy, and extortion for making deals with undercover federal agents to pave the way for introducing slot machines and casino gambling into Washington State.

Early in 1979, the three allegedly told an undercover FBI agent that they would help get gambling legislation passed in return for 18 percent of the gross profits of a phony FBI firm's gambling business.

O'Brien had not seen the scandal coming. He did remember Bagnariol showing up one Monday and enthusing over the California golf course on which he had played that weekend. In retrospect, it was clear he had been playing with FBI agents.

Both legislators protested their innocence. Bagnariol resigned as co-Speaker. Walgren said he would not step down. The jury convicted all three men. One month before a conservative landslide swept Ronald Reagan into the White House, the Gamscam defendants were swept into jail. All three were convicted of racketeering. Bagnariol and Gallagher were also convicted of conspiracy and extortion. The men were sentenced to five years in prison. (Nine years later, a federal appeals court overturned Walgren's racketeering conviction and a conviction for mail fraud. In reversing the latter, it cited a 1987 United States Supreme Court ruling that said the mail fraud statute protected only property rights, *not* intangibles "such as the public right to corruption-free government.")

The Sawyer dynasty had ended. The remainder of the Democratic establishment that succeeded O'Brien had gone out in disgrace. Some legislators had helped elect Bagnariol Speaker three years before because they felt he was the only candidate who could keep things under control. Now he was on his way to jail, and the erosion of the Speaker's authority soon gathered steam.

O'Brien found it ironic that John Bagnariol and Gordon Walgren had gone to jail for allegedly agreeing to pass legislation that would bring big-time gambling to Washington. In his opinion, they had been nailed for promising the impossible. His years in the legislature had convinced him that legislation to permit slot machines and casino gambling would never pass. They had blown their careers for a chimera.

In the meantime, Bagnariol's resignation at the begin-

ning of April had left the Democratic half of the Speakership vacant, and O'Brien, as Speaker pro tem, had
stepped right in. He clearly did not mind. Duane Berentson, who shared the Speakership with him for the remainder of 1980, and who "always found John very easy
to work with . . . a real gentleman," observed, with considerable understatement, that "John enjoys the rostrum
a lot." Nearly forty years after his first election to the House,
more than seventeen years after the coalition had denied
him his fifth Speakership, O'Brien had the gavel again.
Recalling the way O'Brien returned to the rostrum after
the upheavals of 1976 and 1980, Al Bauer said he "re-
minds me of a seasoned sea captain who has made many
cruises, and they fall back on him when they have stormy
seas."

VIII

A Concern for Appearances

FROM THE VERY START, JOHN O'BRIEN LIKED THE marble and oak, the ceremonial space and the ceremonial procedures of the House. Over the years, he tried consistently to augment the prestige and improve the appearance of the chamber. In the late 1970s and early 1980s, his concern for the physical surroundings of legislation put him into the spotlight.

Sometimes, in the 1960s, he seemed to be taking the legislature's side against all comers. In 1965, faced with redistricting and the start of a Republican gubernatorial dynasty, the legislature decided to take care of itself. Legislators wound up tripling their salaries, to $3,600 a year, increasing their per diem payments from $25 to $40, improving their pension plans—a move that Evans vetoed—and talking seriously about creating more working space for themselves. O'Brien, serving as chairman of a bipartisan House Facilities Committee, defended the legislators' actions: "For forty years, we've taken care of all other state agencies," he said. "Now the legislature has top priority." O'Brien suggested that when the public saw its elected representatives dictating letters at their desks or meeting their constituents in hallways, it got a bad impression. In some circles, the Legislative Facilities Committees were referred to derisively as "image committees."

It may have been easy to laugh at the legislators' concern for appearances, but lack of office space was a genuine problem. State government was growing by leaps and bounds. Under Rosellini, state office buildings had started springing up in the area north of Capitol Way. In the capitol, though, most legislators were still doing business at their desks, storing papers in accordian files, calling secretaries to the House and senate floors so that they could dictate letters. House members had to draw keys to single file drawers in the basement. "It's like a prison," O'Brien said.

He also defended the legislators' boosting of their own salaries and their much-criticized attempt to increase pensions. By then he was serving his third term on the National Conference of State Legislative Leaders' executive committee, and he knew what legislators were being paid in other states. Pointing out that in New York and Michigan they got $25,000 a year, he said, "Too many qualified persons do not stay in the legislature because of the personal sacrifice required and the insufficient compensation. This is a loss to the people."

The people did not seem overly concerned. That was, in a way, exactly O'Brien's point. "What concerns many," he said, "is not how the legislators meet their responsibilities to the public, but rather how the public meets its responsibilities to the legislators." (Years later, O'Brien could not believe he had said that. The public's reaction to the legislature had indeed been an issue, he said, but "the public doesn't have any *responsibility* to the legislature.")

He returned to the theme three years later when, as

outgoing president of the National Conference of State Legislative Leaders, he went to Honolulu for the group's annual meeting and the ceremonial casting of a big floral wreath over the side of the battleship *Arizona* at Pearl Harbor. At a press conference, he called for higher legislative salaries "to help alleviate personal problems—to get good men in the legislature." ("That should be 'good men *and women*,'" O'Brien says today, with hindsight. "Of course, we didn't have many women.")

O'Brien's concern for the stature of the legislature was genuine. It went along with his feeling for the dignity of the Speakership, with the basic formality he brought to politics. Photographs of O'Brien at a 1966 meeting of state legislative leaders in Chicago show virtually everyone else looking very casual in shirtsleeves; O'Brien's jacket is off, but the knot of his narrow tie has not been loosened, his tie clip is in place, and, unlike the men around him, he is not smoking. But despite O'Brien's personal formality, he did not insist that other people dress formally. Later in the decade, during a flap over women wearing slacks in the legislature—it started because girl pages had to make deliveries in the snow—O'Brien said that what other people wore was none of his concern.

It was a very short step from caring about the stature of the place to caring what the place looked like. Mary Kay Becker, a Democratic representative of the late 1970s and early 1980s, recalled that "he always wanted the place to look classy, to have things about it that looked classy." In 1979, O'Brien got $200,000 appropriated for murals in the House and senate chambers and galleries. This was not a new idea. The capitol had been designed for artwork, and attempts had been made to raise money for murals ever since 1918. In 1969, O'Brien and Tom Copeland introduced a bill that would have created a special fund to finance works of art in the capitol; it died without a hearing. No consensus had developed in the intervening eight years; O'Brien simply had decided it was time to make another move.

"We had to struggle to get it," he said. "I offered an amendment to the appropriations bill on the floor of the House to appropriate $200,000 for works of art. It lacked the necessary majority. I moved to reconsider, and the second time, it was adopted.

"The strong argument," he explained, "was that most state capitols have artwork depicting some scenes about the history of the states; our state is devoid of any artwork."

That argument did not exactly sweep all before it. Getting the legislature committed to spending money "was very difficult," O'Brien said, "because appropriation for artwork isn't that easy to achieve. Legislators think the money should be spent for other purposes, more dire needs."

The legislators of 1979 were no exception. The majority did not care deeply about art. Still, on April 20, the House voted 66 to 28 for the appropriation. Some legislators voted yes not because they themselves wanted murals on the walls, but because O'Brien did. The senate concurred—after O'Brien made a suitable concession to the key committee chairman. "Hubert Donohue, who was the chairman of the Ways and Means Committee, didn't want to appropriate the money to the legislative arts commission," O'Brien said. "He wanted to have the Department of General Administration handle the artwork. It was all right with me, as long as it was approved."

The state was flush in 1979, so spending $200,000 did

not weigh heavily on legislators' minds. Two years later, the recession had started, pinching pennies was the order of the day, and what remained of O'Brien's appropriation for artwork became a target. Mary Kay Becker, the ranking Democratic member of the Human Services Appropriations Committee, and other Democrats argued that the state should not be spending its money on murals when human services were being cut back. Besides, Becker figured the chamber looked better with blank walls. Given the conservatism of the legislature and the financial pressures of the time, her objections quickly gained support.

"Representative Becker from Bellingham really started it," O'Brien recalled. The House voted to cut off all money for the legislative art project. O'Brien's motion to reconsider lost on a tie. Seattle artist Michael Spafford had already started painting the murals that were to hang in the House. After the vote, O'Brien said, "[Republican] Speaker [Bill] Polk and I went down and looked at the murals. We told Michael Spafford to go ahead and finish what he had."

Spafford completed the murals for the two House galleries—black-and-white panels showing "The Twelve Labors of Hercules"—which were installed in July. He never painted the murals that were to hang at either end of the House chamber.

Even the murals he did paint proved too many for a lot of conservative representatives. Alden Mason's murals for the senate ruffled a few feathers at the time. (Mason's murals evidently did not grow on the senators over the years. In 1987, the senate voted to take them down.) Spafford's immediately became a *cause célèbre*.

"They've been called everything from 'a pile of garbage' to a 'landmark,'" wrote *Seattle Times* art critic Sue Ann Kendall that November. She explained that Spafford himself viewed the labors of Hercules as "a metaphor for the legislative process" and for "a constant possibility of experiencing defeat."

Legislators did not object to his view of the legislative process; they objected to his style. The designs had been selected by an independent jury. The result was a classic clash between the taste of people in the arts community—who had made up the jury—and popular taste. "The sixty-four-dollar question," O'Brien said, "is whether this type of artwork is really suitable for that chamber." Many legislators felt it was not—and they felt that the attempt to foist it on them had been rather high-handed.

For O'Brien's seventieth birthday, On November 22, the House met in a Sunday session. Unbeknownst to O'Brien—but not to anyone else—the murals had been adorned with pink ribbons, green cellophane, old clothes, and gloves. The galleries were packed. The press was there. O'Brien sat down at his desk in the front row, unaware that anything special was going on. When people couldn't stand it any longer, someone told him to look up.

A doggerel poem composed in O'Brien's honor and signed by every member of the House and Senate read in part:

> He's worked for a minimum salary.
> We think he's a saint,
> But art critic he ain't,
> Cause look what he's done to the gallery!

A lot of House members enjoyed teasing O'Brien about the artwork, Becker explained, because "everyone saw the murals and their theme as being totally at odds with strait-laced John O'Brien."

Not all the reaction was good-natured. O'Brien may have been taken aback by the vehemence of some of it, but the murals' lack of popularity was no surprise. He preferred realistic art, and frankly, he had not been crazy about the murals. Before he had seen the mock-ups, his secretary had said, "Well, you're not going to like it." It was not what he had expected. He commented later that his reaction to the jury-approved design "was sort of negative, and Spafford told me one day in the Speaker's office, 'This isn't the type of artwork you had in mind, is it?' I said, 'Well, no.' We thought we'd have four panels describing, oh, the history of the state, the economy, resources. We went along with it, though. We didn't have much choice. Maybe it wasn't totally suitable for the chambers, but it was better than nothing."

That was not the prevailing sentiment. Early in 1982 conservatives launched an effort to get the murals covered or removed. Representative Michael Patrick, a former Seattle vice squad cop, argued that the murals met all three tests of pornography: they had no redeeming social value; they appealed to prurient interest; and they were an affront to community standards. Representative Dick Nelson replied to Patrick: "If you see anything strange, perhaps it's in the eyes or mind of the beholder."

Perhaps it was, but a lot of the beholders had similar eyes and minds. "Bill Polk was very much in favor of the murals," O'Brien said, "but the whole Republican caucus got very worked up over them. He couldn't do anything with them. They were very conservative. He couldn't reason with them. They wanted to take the murals down; sell them."

Polk himself—who thought some of Spafford's work was "dynamite" but considered the murals too stark—said later,

"My informal polling told me that about 90 percent of the House wanted them out." Nonetheless, many Democrats would continue to vote for the murals out of deference to O'Brien.

The conservatives and other hostile legislators succeeded in getting the murals placed out of sight and more or less out of mind. A front-page headline in the *Seattle Post-Intelligencer* of March 8 announced, "HOUSE VOTES TO GET RID OF 'DIRTY' MURALS." Spafford's wife said that the legislators "are so peculiar, so literal, so anti-art and anti-education. They see things that aren't."

Only O'Brien, Polk, and Spafford himself knew that the legislators could have been made a great deal more upset. When O'Brien first saw Spafford's work, "in the first panel, he had [pictured] the testicles of Hercules. I asked, 'What's that?' He said, 'The balls of Hercules.' I said, 'Get rid of them.'"

So the murals were covered over. The incident—and certainly the rhetoric it evoked—seemed to say a lot about the conservatism of the House in the early 1980s. But maybe appearances were deceiving. Six years later, the executive rules committee of a much less conservative House voted to get rid of the murals entirely. By the time it was over, O'Brien had acquired a reputation as a champion of modern art.

Another art project in the late 1970s had a happier outcome. In fact, O'Brien was to consider it one of the proudest achievements of his long career. Al Bauer and other legislators from the Vancouver area had sponsored a bill that would designate a Catholic nun, Mother Joseph, as the subject of Washington's second statue in Statuary Hall in the United States Capitol. Each state is entitled to two statues, each portraying an individual who played a crucial role in the development of the state. In 1953, Washington installed a statue of pioneer missionary Marcus Whitman. During America's bicentennial celebration in 1976, a group of people in Vancouver started pushing for a statue of Mother Joseph. They sent O'Brien their literature. Since his old friend, Sister Agnes, belonged to Mother Joseph's order, the Sisters of Providence, he was interested.

Mother Joseph led a group of Sisters of Providence from Montreal to Washington Territory in 1856. That year, she designed and supervised the construction of Providence Academy in Vancouver. Over the next forty-four years, she was responsible for building twenty-eight more institutions, primarily schools and hospitals, in the Northwest. She built Providence Hospital in Seattle, St. Peter's Hospital in Olympia, and Sacred Heart Hospital in Spokane. The West Coast Lumbermen's Association later designated her "the first white artisan to work with wood in the Pacific Northwest." In 1953, the American Institute of Architects declared her "the First Architect of the Pacific Northwest."

"I think she was a very strong individual with a sense of objectives and urgency and a desire to achieve things," O'Brien said. "I think she was the kind of person who didn't hesitate to go out and ask for money to achieve her objectives."

When the time came to introduce a bill to authorize a statue of Mother Joseph, Bauer enlisted O'Brien as a secondary sponsor. The bill quickly got bogged down in the House Rules Committee. Knowing that Washington was entitled to only one more statue, some representatives wanted to save the space for Warren Magnuson. Some just wanted to save it for someone who was not a religious figure. O'Brien got it out of the Rules Committee and helped move it through the House. Then the senate sat on it. The senate passed its own version of a Mother Joseph bill and sent it to the House. Again, it got stuck in the Rules Committee. Again, O'Brien placed it on the calendar and pushed it through the House.

The bill passed both houses, but then Bauer was warned that the governor might veto it. She had been urged to save the place in Statuary Hall for someone else. Bauer phoned Governor Ray. She told him yes, she had been approached about vetoing the bill. Bauer asked to talk with her. He took O'Brien along. "O'Brien really leaned on her," he recalled. Not only did Ray not veto the bill; she became an enthusiastic supporter.

Once the bill was signed into law, Bauer said, "O'Brien took over." The project's appeal went beyond aesthetics: a Mother Joseph statue would get unusual recognition for a Catholic heroine and would get O'Brien himself recognition from the Catholic Church. He threw himself into it.

The legislation established a committee to raise money from private donations for the statue. The Speaker of the House was to be a member of the committee. Bagnariol was not interested, so he appointed O'Brien, the Speaker pro tem, to serve in his place. The committee was set up as the Mother Joseph Foundation, and O'Brien became its chairman.

The Mother Joseph Foundation chose an internationally known sculptor of public works, Felix de Welden, to sculpt Mother Joseph. De Welden had created the Iwo Jima flag-raising memorial in Washington, D.C. His image of Mother Joseph is in a very different vein. While most of the figures in Statuary Hall are predictably heroic, standing tall and staring off into the future, perhaps with an arm upraised, Mother Joseph, as De Welden has cast her, is kneeling, looking up toward heaven. O'Brien was much impressed by this departure from the norm and by the fact that de Welden had envisioned it in a dream. He found de Welden, like other artists, attractive and a bit inscrutable.

In October 1980, O'Brien presided over ceremonies in the state capitol; the Mother Joseph Foundation presented replicas of the Mother Joseph statue and the earlier statue of Marcus Whitman to the state of Washington. That May, less than a month after O'Brien became acting Speaker in the aftermath of the Gamscam scandal, he flew to Washington, D.C., for the unveiling and formal acceptance of the original Mother Joseph statue.

In her letter to him afterward, Governor Ray said, "I appreciate all you did to make a dream come true. Many persons told me it was by far the best organized and most impressive dedication of a Statuary Hall entry in the long history of that famous place. You have helped make us all proud. . . . Without your efforts it could not have happened."

The ceremony took place in the Capitol rotunda, under the dome; the great circular room was filled with people. Before the ceremony, "we met in a room [outside the rotunda,]" O'Brien said, "and the sergeant at arms, who was a former Notre Dame football star, called my name. We went down one of the long corridors, and all of a sudden we were in the rotunda. There were television cameras all around the place, and it was just packed." As master of ceremonies, O'Brien introduced the Speaker of the United

States House of Representatives, Thomas P. (Tip) O'Neill, Washington's two United States Senators, Warren Magnuson and Henry Jackson, Governor Dixy Lee Ray, the Superior General of the Sisters of Providence, and the Vatican's delegate to the United States. It was perhaps the most gratifying moment of his public life.

IX

Always Speaker in His Heart

THE EARLY 1980S WERE BAD YEARS FOR WASHINGTON Democrats, and almost disastrous years for John O'Brien. But he had not lost his political will, and he did not lose the House seat that meant so much to him.

By the time the legislature met in 1981, the recession of the early 1980s had started. Demand for housing was plummeting, dragging the state's forest products industry down with it. Unemployment was rising rapidly. Tax revenues were not keeping up with the demand for social services.

The legislature that had to deal with the state's economic problems was unusually conservative. In the Reagan landslide of 1980, Washington elected a Republican governor, John Spellman, and a Republican majority in the House. A number of the House Republicans elected in 1980 stood a good deal to the right of their Speaker, Bill Polk. The senate had gone Democratic by one seat, but—in a move that evoked as much outrage as the coalition of 1963—one Democratic senator, Pete von Reichbauer, switched parties in midstream, giving the Republicans control of both houses.

By 1982, with statewide unemployment at 12.5 percent,

the Republican majority was willing to try just about anything to put some money into the state's coffers. Spending cuts would not suffice. At the end of the 1982 session, with the help of a handful of Democrats eager to pass something and go home, they restored the sales tax on food, which the people had removed by initiative. They voted in a state lottery bill, which legislatures had been summarily rejecting for decades.

O'Brien joined the majority of Democrats in futile votes against these bills. He did not stop them. He did, however, succeed in slowing down the Republican juggernaut more than once. "He's brilliant," recalled a young Democratic staff member of the early 1980s. "He got the caucus out of more scrapes by making parliamentary deals."

O'Brien himself was pleased that by raising points of order he was able to slow things down, to make the Republicans stop and caucus so they could figure out their next moves. "We had a very friendly warfare on parliamentary procedure," recalled Bill Polk. "I learned a lot from him. We also got a great deal of joy out of looking up John O'Brien decisions [on House rules] over the years on both sides of every issue." The Republicans would look until they found an O'Brien decision that would allow them to do what they wanted.

Despite the parliamentary maneuvering, Polk appreciated the civilizing influence exerted by O'Brien's knowledge of and insistence on the correct forms. It was, he said, "the kind of thing that made the place livable when people were a little testy."

O'Brien could not influence the course of legislation, but he did come up with two of the biennium's better one-liners. The legislature started scrambling to get control of the budget in 1981. The House majority decided to underfund pensions, delay school funding, and borrow money from the school construction fund. O'Brien said, "Father, forgive them, for they know not what they do." On October 18, President Reagan admitted for the first time that there was a recession. The next month, when the legislature met in a special session to deal with the state's financial crisis, O'Brien had grown a bit less charitable. The House had voted to reduce public school spending by 1 percent and to delay a pay raise for state workers. It had also passed a one-cent increase in the sales tax. O'Brien quipped—referring to Reagan's "trickle-down" economics in which tax breaks and incentives for people on the highest rungs of the economic ladder were supposed to stimulate the economy enough to help people lower down—that the Republican plan "doesn't trickle down; it just down-and-outs a lot of people."

The Republicans found themselves controlling both houses and the governor's office at just the right time: after the 1980 census, the state was due to redistrict again. For the first time in living memory, the legislature did it without being pressed. The majority had no reason not to. The Republicans could do largely as they pleased. And they did, turning the job over to conservative Bob Eberle. Legislative districts were redrawn with the Republicans' welfare in mind.

The neutral redistricting of 1972 had not hurt O'Brien at all. Opposed only by an independent, he had won by a margin of 8,434 to 448. This time was different. O'Brien's district, which had changed from the 33rd to the 35th back in 1965, now became the 37th, and it took in different ground. The area had changed over the past forty years, anyway. Following a familiar pattern of urban evolution, many of the old Irish and Italian families had moved to the suburbs, and people with different ethnic backgrounds had moved in. Redistricting accelerated this shift in O'Brien's constituency.

He never stopped being close to the Catholic Church or representing Catholic interests. In 1985, Father D. Harvey McIntyre, executive director of the Washington State Catholic Conference, said O'Brien was "always in tune with the Church." Conference lobbyist Sister Sharon Park said, "He drops everything to listen to us."

These endorsements meant less than they would have years before. Where once O'Brien could score points with Irish and Italian constituents by sponsoring legislation that would let parochial school children ride public school buses, now he had to deal with mail from Asian constituents about a bill to regulate acupuncture.

He still had Catholic constituents, still represented people with Irish or Italian roots, but suddenly his legislative district was more than half nonwhite. Many of its residents had not spent the past four decades thinking of him as their man in Olympia. If ever there was a perfect time to knock off John O'Brien, the 1982 election, right after the redistricting, seemed to be it.

Some people were eager to try. Two strong candidates ran against O'Brien in the Democratic primary, and he found himself with little more than one-third of the vote. His two opponents split the majority votes, though, and he got more than either of them. Since the new district was no more inclined to vote Republican than the old one had been, the primary victory left him secure for another term. The same thing happened in 1984.

If luck held for O'Brien in 1984, it ran out for his old antagonists at Washington Water Power. Early in the year, Bob Perry, who had already pleaded guilty to income tax evasion and extortion, turned up as the star witness in the trial of his old employer, Washington Water Power. Also on trial were its chief lobbyist, Jerry Buckley; and the Sergeant–Tyee Construction Company, Washington Water Power's alleged accomplice in the laundering of money. Buckley and his company were charged with mail fraud for mailing state disclosure forms that did not reflect the money laundered through Hong Kong to pay off state legislators in the mid-1970s. They were also charged with obstruction of justice for helping Perry skip the country to avoid testifying at Robert Gulino's perjury trial in 1977. At the trial, an assistant U.S. attorney said, "The real villain is not Mr. Sergeant or Mr. Buckley. The real villain is Washington Water Power." Nevertheless, Buckley was convicted and sentenced to jail. O'Brien, who by then was not inclined to speak ill of anyone, claimed to feel sorry for him. (Buckley's fraud conviction, which carried a jail sentence, was later overturned for lack of evidence. The obstruction of justice conviction stood.)

By that time, Washington State, like the rest of the country, had left the recession of the early 1980s behind. (Urban Washington had, anyway. Farmers still battled low prices and the towns of the coast and mountains remained chronically depressed.) The conservative legislature of the early 1980s was already history. A Democrat, Booth Gardner, was elected governor in 1984. When the legislative session began in 1985, O'Brien was elected to his sixth term as Speaker pro tem.

The next year, he ran his twenty-fourth campaign for the House. Only a single opponent faced him in the primary. Both the *Seattle Times* and *The Weekly* endorsed his opponent. O'Brien ran what was in some ways a very old-fashioned campaign. He knew that the surest way to get something done was to do it oneself, so when his mailers needed address labels stuck on, he took them down to the direct-mail house himself, piling them in the trunk and back seat of his car. (He never had liked depending too much on other people. Even after the legislature acquired a full-time staff, O'Brien continued to do a lot of his own research on bills.) His supporters got the yard signs out.

He had already mended his political fences. Before, he may have grown a bit remote from the concerns of his district; now, in the past two years, he had shown a variety of constituents that he cared about their issues. He had allied himself with the people who were fighting to keep the Seattle School District from tearing down the facade of old Franklin High School, successfully urging the district to demolish only the interior and build a new school in the shell of the old. At the request of three rabbis from his district, he had successfully sponsored one of the first statutes in the nation that required any food sold as "kosher" or "kosher-style" to be genuine kosher; at the signing, O'Brien, the classic Irish politician, posed with the governor and four bearded rabbis in traditional hats. After receiving a petition with 300 names on it, he had worked to keep the state Department of Transportation from eliminating all off ramps into his district while it replaced the old I-90 highway into downtown Seattle. His work on the I-90 off ramps won him the support of black businessmen who would have suffered financially if the district were cut off, and of other constituents who did not relish the prospect of driving west in order to reach the highway heading east. In the primary, O'Brien won 65 percent of the Democratic vote. In November, he was re-elected with 84 percent. His years of close calls seemed over. The House elected him Speaker pro tem once again.

His classes in parliamentary procedure for freshman leg-
islators were videotaped for posterity; they would become
House references, like *Reed's Rules of Order* or *Mason's
Precedents*.

Much had changed since O'Brien was the ambitious first-
term legislator elected to a House in which providing pensions to the aged was the big issue. For that matter, much
had changed since O'Brien was the Speaker with a quick
gavel and an encyclopedic knowledge of the rules presiding over battles between public and private power.

People no longer saw his partisan edge. During the tough
primary fight of 1984, Doug Underwood of the *Seattle Times*
wrote that "O'Brien, the legendary House Speaker of the
1950s, has evolved from the hot-tempered leader who ruled
with an iron grip into a gentle elder statesman who pre-
sides without controversy. . . . 'The ceremony has become more important to him than the power,' one Democratic staffer observed. While O'Brien still attends
legislative leadership meetings, he plays little role in the
backroom decision-making, according to legislative insiders." O'Brien disliked Underwood's article intensely.

It was true that presiding had come to be something
O'Brien enjoyed for its own sake rather than as a means
to partisan ends. It was true that O'Brien himself had said,
"I like to preside and be part of the action. As Senator
Magnuson said to me one time back in the United States
Senate, 'You know, John, if we weren't doing this, we'd
miss it.'" It was true that he had always enjoyed the trap-
pings of leadership: the big office just off the floor of the
House, the good parking spot in the capitol basement. At
the same time, he was in many ways frugal with the taxpayers' money. When he called home from Olympia, he
reversed the charges. His long-time secretary noted that

he "never had fancy fish" in his office like one former Speaker, or "aides who lit cigarettes for him" like another.

And it was true that O'Brien had become known for an enigmatic smile. Some younger legislators took that smile as evidence that he had seen it all before, or perhaps that he often did not care. The fact was, though, that Democrats had noted that same enigmatic smile while O'Brien sat in the eye of the stormy 1963 session, after the coalition had denied him his fifth term as Speaker.

And the fact was that he had not lost sight of what was happening in the House. Powerful legislators still said that he knew everything that was going on, and that while he let a lot go by, if he chose to get involved, he knew how to help—or hurt—a bill. Mark Brown, lobbyist for the Washington Federation of State Employees, told the *Seattle Times* that O'Brien "still wields considerable clout in the legislature. When he gets involved, he gets results." He certainly had not gone soft. "The word no isn't in his vocabulary," an admirer said, "unless *he's* using it." When people asked for his help, O'Brien still did things for Seattle. He had introduced the bill that enabled the city to charge admission to the annual Seafair Hydroplane Races on Lake Washington—providing badly needed funds for cleanup and security—and had introduced the initial, unsuccessful bill to establish the State Convention and Trade Center.

O'Brien never saw himself as just another member of the caucus. In 1985, some independent service station owners pushed a bill that would have prevented large oil companies from operating gas stations. The oil companies opposed it. Each side claimed the other's program would eventually cost the consumer money. The bill's first big hurdle was the House Rules Committee, which could keep it from reaching the floor. O'Brien and Democratic Speaker Wayne Ehlers were both members of Rules. In a closed Democratic caucus meeting, Ehlers asked the other Democrats how he should vote. The caucus instructed him to vote for the bill. Ehlers did. O'Brien did not. O'Brien was one of two Democrats who voted with the seven Republicans on the Rules Committee and kept the bill off the floor. "The Speaker voted for it, but I didn't," O'Brien said. "He asked for the caucus vote, but I didn't. I didn't ask the caucus to tell *me* how to vote."

John O'Brien realized long ago that battles over specific bills—and most of the bills themselves—are transient phenomena. What he or any other legislator has done to pass or kill any particular bill will not be long remembered, except perhaps by political insiders and newspaper columnists. But the process and the physical setting of legislation will endure. The rules O'Brien has made will guide legislative debate in Washington State during the next century. The statuary he has put in the capitol may endure longer than that.

The scene will stay the same: anyone who climbs the forty-five marble steps to the state capitol, walks through the impressive columns, passes through the glass doors that cover bronze doors bearing reliefs of landscape, explorers, and pioneers, and enters the building can glance right and see a statue of Marcus Whitman in a buckskin suit and coonskin cap, a thick Bible in his right hand, saddle bags in his left, striding toward tomorrow. On the left, Mother Joseph kneels in prayer, a cross around her neck, her long dress a study in drapery. Her upturned face, her hands pressed together look too strong and capable to be those of a supplicant. Against the far wall, to the left of the three doorways that lead a visitor up under the dome, a bronze plaque is affixed at eye level. It says: "Statues of Mother Joseph and Marcus Whitman presented to the state of Washington by Mother Joseph Foundation, the Honorable John L. O'Brien, Chairman of the board of directors, 1980."

The statues and the plaque are of bronze. They will last. The House Office Building, which O'Brien's colleagues voted on St. Patrick's Day 1989 to rename the John L. O'Brien Building, will last too, as will the John L. O'Brien Postgraduate Legislative Fellowships, established in his honor by his legislative colleagues for graduates of Washington state colleges who want to study government firsthand. Another legacy is the awarding of the Washington State Medals of Merit, which John O'Brien initiated.

People who have watched Speakers in the past, though, will remember O'Brien for more than the bronzes or the building or the medals—or the gala parties at which he dispenses Irish coffee to hundreds of people every St. Patrick's Day when the legislature is in session. They will remember him first of all for his style on the rostrum. Jim Dwyer, who went to Olympia as caucus attorney in 1973 and saw O'Brien preside as Speaker pro tem, remembers him as "an artist" on the rostrum. Mary Kay Becker, who started the fight against the murals, says, "he is more *graceful* than anyone else I've ever seen . . . He really has provided a lot of elegance."

And they will remember his personal integrity. Unlike some onetime colleagues and rivals, O'Brien has never been linked to shady associates or shady practices. Payton Smith, who served as Speaker's attorney during the tumultuous session of 1961, remembers that "he always expected people to do the right thing. He was always disappointed when they didn't." During a time at which many legislators were identified with special interests or were considered for sale, Smith found O'Brien "absolutely incorruptible."

Julia Butler Hansen, O'Brien's House colleague of the 1940s and 1950s, appreciated the fact that "he was always common sense. You could always talk to him, reason with him." She considered him "a very good legislator [who has] never gotten over being Speaker. The Speakership has always been magic to him. [He has loved] the mechanics, the ceremony, and the rules."

Other politicians have seen the Speakership as a stepping stone, an interlude, at most a brief moment of glory. O'Brien has been obsessed by it during most of his adult life. And, of course, O'Brien has mastered the process of presiding in a way that has won the respect of opponents as well as allies. Slade Gorton, who entered the House when O'Brien was at his peak of power in the late 1950s, says, "he still remains in my mind as the model of an efficient and effective presiding officer. . . . I have never, from that day to this, observed a better one."

Gorton feels, though, that during the epic battle between public and private power in 1961, O'Brien "operated in a way that I think is safe to say [was] unfair. . . . That rather arbitrary use of power led inevitably to his replacement."

The coalition of 1963 that cost O'Brien his fifth Speakership certainly has loomed large in his own memory. But he has grown philosophical about it. "The legislature is like being involved in a contest," he says. "You go out on the floor of the House and you do the best you can. The roll call may go for you or the vote may go against you. It's just one of those things. But then, after it's over, you consider other issues. You don't get disturbed because something happened. It might stay with you for a while, but as far as being disappointed—you can't let it remain as a personal matter. Because there's always another roll call, there's always another day."

Chronology

LEGISLATIVE LEADERSHIP ROLES

Speaker of the House—4 terms   1955 to 1963—8 years

Acting Speaker   1976, 1980—2 years

Speaker Pro Tempore—7 terms   1973 to 1981—8 years
                                      1983 to 1988—6 years

Majority Leader and Caucus
    Chairman   1951 to 1953—2 years

Minority Floor Leader   1953 to 1955—2 years

Democratic Floor Leader   1963 to 1965—2 years

Majority Leader   1965 to 1967—2 years

Minority Leader   1967 to 1971—4 years

Chairman, Minority Executive
    Committee   1971 to 1973—2 years

Democratic Parliamentary Leader   1981 to 1983—2 years

President of the National
    Conference
of State Legislative Leaders   1968

Vice President of the National
    Conference
of State Legislative Leaders   1967

Member of Executive Committee
    of National
Conference of Legislative Leaders   1962 to 1974—13 years

Chairman, Washington State
    Legislative Council   1955 to 1963—8 years

Secretary, Washington State
    Legislative Council   1953 to 1955—2 years

Member of Washington State
    House of
Representatives; appointed
    October 1939 to fill
an unexpired term; did not serve
    1947–1949   1939 to 1989—48 years

Afterword: Sources and Acknowledgments

WRITTEN ACCOUNTS OF THE PAST HALF-CEN-
tury's politics in Washington State are hard to come by.
Not only is there a dearth of published history, but the
House and senate journals for most of that period record
virtually nothing except the subjects of bills and the vote
tallies. Consequently, my main sources of information have
been the memories of participants and observers and the
political reporting of two daily newspapers, the *Seattle Post-
Intelligencer* and the *Seattle Times*.

John L. O'Brien shared many of his recollections with
me in a series of taped interviews that we began in late
1985 and continued into 1987. He also shared his personal scrapbooks of newspaper clippings. In addition, I
consulted the John L. O'Brien Collection in the Archives
of the University of Washington Library.

However limited their usefulness, I did consult the House
journals for those years. I also consulted the records of
the Legislative Council, which are in the Washington State
Archives in Olympia, the published records of the Canwell Committee, the nonconfidential portions of O'Brien's
candidate file at the Municipal League of Seattle and King
County, and the court files on the federal prosecutions of

Robert Perry and Robert Gulino. Ken Billington, former director of the Washington Public Utility Districts Association and long-time public utility lobbyist, made available chapters of his then-unpublished autobiography, *People, Politics, and Public Power* (Washington Public Utilities Districts Association, 1988).

Other sources include: taped interviews with former Speaker Charles Hodde, published by the office of Washington's secretary of state in 1985; Clarence C. Dill's self-published 1970 autobiography, *Where the Water Falls;* Gordon Newell's anecdotal history of the legislature, *Rogues, Buffoons, and Statesmen* (Superior, 1975); Vern Countryman's account of the Canwell phenomenon, *Un-American Activities, Washington Style* (Cornell University Press, 1951); and *Public Policymaking, Washington Style* by Hugh A. Bone, Nand E. Hard Nibbrig and Robert H. Pealy (Institute of Government Relations, University of Washington, 1980).

Individuals who contributed information and, in many cases, perspective, include: Charles Hodde; Ken Billington; the late State Representative and Congresswoman Julia Butler Hansen; former Speaker Mort Frayn; former Governor Albert Rosellini; former state Representative and Attorney General (now U.S. Senator) Slade Gorton; the late journalist Ross Cunningham; James Ellis, who both conceived of and lobbied for Metro; former state Democratic Chairman Herb Legg; former Legislative Council staff counsel and veteran Olympia lobbyist Bob Seeber; former Speaker's attorney Payton Smith; former Democratic caucus attorney Jim Dwyer; former administrative assistant to Dan Evans (now state supreme court justice) Jim Dolliver; former Seattle city lobbyist Bob Gogerty; the late environmental activist Tom Wimmer; Assistant Attorney General Charles Roe; political consultant Wally

Toner; former Puget Power President Ralph Davis; and Ed Guthman, who covered the Canwell Committee excesses and the Canwell hearing for the *Seattle Times*. I spoke with many current or former state legislators, including Bob Greive, Ray Olsen, Fred Dore, Dave Sprague, Duane Berentson, Sam Smith, Ed Munro, Brian Ebersole, Helen Sommers, Dan Grimm, Denny Heck, Rick Bender, John McKibbin, Al Bauer, Jim Boldt, Bill Polk, and Mary Kay Becker.

Chapter 1. The descriptions of James O'Brien's death, which vary from one account to another, are taken mainly from the *Seattle Post-Intelligencer* of January 23, 1921. The description of Olympia when the legislature opened in 1941 relies heavily on an article by Virginia Boren in the *Seattle Times* of January 13, 1941. The description of the legislative debate over helping Britain comes from Gordon Newell. Background information about Depression-era efforts at tax reform comes from Charles Hodde.

Chapter 2. Background material on the Canwell Committee episode comes from Vern Countryman. Details about Charles Hodde securing the Speakership for 1949 were provided by Hodde himself.

Chapter 3. Clarence Dill's 1970 autobiography lays out the plan to do away with Washington Water Power. Details of the bribery incident appeared in the Seattle press and in the House journal. O'Brien catching former Speaker Ed Reilly on a parliamentary fine point was described to me by Ken Billington.

Chapter 4. Descriptions of the Canwell Committee hearing are from the Seattle press and from John O'Brien.

Chapter 5. The change in lobbying techniques was described to me by Bob Seeber.

Chapter 8. My account of the revolt against Leonard Sawyer derives from conversations with the legislators who were involved.

Chapter 10. Information about O'Brien's 1986 campaign was supplied by Wally Toner.

Index